T0274570

Empower Your Life Through Feng Shui

An easy eight-step guide to help you achieve your goals

Maria McCullough

Rights and Permissions:
Western School of Feng Shui- Terah Kathryn Collins - obtained permissions to
use graphs and charts

Maria McCullough
Book Baby Publishing
Pennsauken Township, New Jersey
www.Fengshuibymaria.com

Ordering Information:
For details, contact - Book Baby https://www.bookbaby.com

Print ISBN: 979-8-35093-947-7
Printed in the United States of America on SFI Certified paper.
First Edition

Dedicated to my two greatest loves:

My beautiful daughter, Katrina, who has lent her extraordinary and unique talents to the making of this book, and my loving husband, John, whose love, confidence, and continual support have made writing this book possible.

You both have been my biggest supporters through my journey into Feng Shui.

I send blessings to you every day.

Contents

Preface

"Mrs. McCullough, can I paint my classroom green?" was the question that changed my life twenty-five years ago and introduced me to Feng Shui.

At the time, I was principal of an elementary school, and the fifth-grade teacher had approached me with this request. Little did she know that at that moment she became the catalyst of an inspiration that would transform my life and those of many others.

Having no problem with the painting project, I queried her on the purpose. She began to describe the art of Feng Shui; her practitioner, Michelle Cox; and the calming effect that a green classroom would have on her active fifth graders.

Thus began my journey into this fascinating new way of viewing reality. I read numerous books on the subject and invited Michelle Cox to bless my home and do a Feng Shui consultation. You see, my husband of seven years and I were in transition. We had separated four months earlier and through counseling were in the process of reuniting, purchasing a new home, and starting fresh. Years later, I would tell my Feng Shui students that Feng Shui is especially helpful during transitions.

We hired Michelle to bless and enhance our new home, we renewed our vows with a minister before friends in our living room, and with Feng Shui practices as support, we have now celebrated our thirty-fifth year together and look forward to many more. *Feng Shui works!*

Over the years, Feng Shui principles have guided us, not only in the continual enhancement of all areas of our home but also in the enhancement of our offices. Colleagues have walked into my office, sat down, and commented on the positive feeling it evokes. I have been successful in my career, have earned numerous awards and promotions, and was able to retire from my administrative position well over ten years ago.

My goal upon retirement was to continue my rewarding journey into Feng Shui professionally to share what I'd learned with others. To that end, I attended the Western School of Feng Shui™ Practitioner's Institute and was trained by the legendary Terah Kathryn Collins, creator of the Western School of Feng Shui™ and author of numerous books. I became a certified Feng Shui consultant and opened my new business, www.fengshuibymaria.com. I now teach classes; write columns for various newspapers; and hold many in-home and virtual home and business consultations, both nationally and internationally.

How fulfilling it is for me to see clients happy and successful! They have found love, increased their prosperity, and discovered renewed energy and bliss in their lives. This can happen for you, too. I will take you step by step through the process.

Let's get started!

Introduction

People often ask, "What is Feng Shui, really?" and "How can I do it?"

The ancient Chinese art of Feng Shui explores the connection between you and your environment and is the study of how to arrange your environment to enhance your life. It is NOT a mystery. Your environment is here to support you, and when it is uncluttered, peaceful, beautiful, and filled with positive memories, it allows you to center yourself and relax. In a happy and relaxed state you can be more open to opportunities that come your way. An environment that is arranged with intention following Feng Shui principles will support you in achieving your life goals.

Feng Shui, which means *"Wind and Water,"* originated in China more than three thousand years ago when early Chinese Feng Shui practitioners began exploring nature to locate the most secure and stable places to live. Ultimately, they determined that the most favorable locations were those that offered physical protection at their backs, somewhere between the top of a mountain, which they found too windy and precarious, and the base, which was prone to flooding. Eventually they settled in areas that were midway between the wind and the water. In their search for desirable living conditions, they discovered that some areas held more positive energy than others. To understand why, they studied patterns in nature and observed that five basic elements—Water, Wood, Fire, Earth, and Metal—made up the natural world and existed in a continuous nourishing cycle of creation: Water nurtured wood, wood fed fire, fire burned down to ash to make earth, earth turned into stone which made metal, and metal could be made to hold water. These elements later became known as the Five Feng Shui Elements. The early practitioners observed that when all five of these elements were present together and balanced, they produced a harmonious flow of positive energy, which they referred to as Ch'i, the vital life force that exists in and around everything.

They also observed nature's opposite yet complementary energy forces, such as light/dark, hot/cold, old/young, female/male, which they called Yin (expressions of female energy) and Yang (expressions of male energy). The optimum environment, they concluded, balanced both Yin and Yang energy and the energy of the Five Elements. Seeing how this balance of earth's elements and forces encouraged the flow of Ch'i in natural environments, the early Feng Shui practitioners studied ways to apply the same principles in their homes.

They created a grid map with eight sectors around a center to mark the areas in the home that represented what they believed were the most significant areas of one's life:

1. Career
2. Knowledge and Self-Cultivation
3. Health, Family, and Friends
4. Wealth and Prosperity
5. Fame and Reputation
6. Love, Marriage, and Relationships
7. Children and Creativity
8. Helpful People and Travel
9. Center and Grounding

They called this map the "Bagua," which originates from the *I Ching* or *Book of Changes* and literally means "eight trigrams." The ninth sector, the Center, is the hub of the home and the area that grounds and energizes the surrounding areas of the Bagua. The early practitioners believed that the physical arrangement of the Bagua areas in their homes corresponded to the quality of these areas in their lives.

From the ancient teachings of the early practitioners we have learned that Feng Shui can be applied to the home environment in simple steps. The first is to place the Bagua over the layout of the home to locate the areas that correspond to the Bagua's nine sectors. The next is to make "enhancements" to these areas, such as clearing clutter, arranging items with intention, and balancing the Five Elements and Yin Yang Energy to draw the Ch'i into the space and support its flow.

Whether you realize it or not, your home environment either supports or drains your life energy. Making a few simple changes in your home can have an immediate and powerful effect on your personal well-being, as well as on the material aspects of your life. I call it empowerment through environment! You create a supportive environment for yourself by decluttering and enhancing the spaces in your home to help circulate the Ch'i.

Over the years I have found that some of my clients are overwhelmed when trying to make changes in their home and don't know where to start. So, being a believer in accomplishing big tasks a little at a time, I have developed an easy system for enhancing one's home environment one area at a time, in eight manageable steps that will help you to internalize Feng Shui principles and give you what I call "Feng Shui eyes."

Eight Steps to Achieving Your Goals

1. Map out your home using the Bagua.
2. Evaluate your needs and life goals (more love, health, prosperity, career, etc.).
3. Analyze your home's Bagua map and prioritize an area you have the greatest need to improve.
4. Clean and declutter your area of greatest need.
5. Enhance your area of greatest need and write affirmations of your goals.
6. Anchor "missing" areas outside the Bagua map or the structure itself.
7. Create a vision board that depicts your goals.
8. Balance the Five Elements and Yin Yang Energy.

You will feel the energy shift as soon as you begin!

Clients have asked if they can enhance more than one area of the Bagua map at a time in steps three through five. My purpose in suggesting that you begin by prioritizing one area of greatest need and focusing on your goals in that area is to keep the process manageable. Once you have enhanced your first area of need and feel the shift in energy, you will find it easier to move to the next Bagua areas you want to improve.

In workbook fashion, I have included questions at the end of each chapter (Your Turn) to help you reflect on the current state of your life, the goals you want to achieve to make it better, and ways you can apply Feng Shui principles in your home to help you achieve your goals. Your written responses will serve as a useful guide as you begin to practice the art of arranging your home to enhance and empower your life.

Chapter 1:
Step 1 - Map Out Your Home Using the Bagua

You are in control!

If you are like me, you enjoy the ability to control most aspects of your life. I struggled with this for years until I became aware of the ancient Chinese art of empowerment through environment. With Feng Shui I learned to recognize the impact my environment had on my life and how I could make it work constructively for me. You too can work with your environment to empower your life. Balancing your lifestyle and arranging your home to allow it to hold happiness are two vital components of Feng Shui.

WEALTH PROSPERITY	FAME REPUTATION	LOVE MARRIAGE RELATIONSHIPS
HEALTH FAMILY FRIENDS	CENTER GROUNDING	CHILDREN CREATIVITY
KNOWLEDGE SELF-CULTIVATION	CAREER	HELPFUL PEOPLE AND TRAVEL

↑   ↑   ↑

ENTRANCE QUADRANT

How to Use the Bagua

The first step in my eight-step plan is to use the Bagua map to locate the areas of your home that fall within each of the nine sectors. This is crucial to understanding how your home environment affects your life. (While references in this book will be related to the home, all my recommendations can also be applied to a business.)

Prior to every in-person consultation I do, I ask my clients to send me a picture of either an architectural drawing of the layout of their home or a drawing they've sketched out by hand so that I can lay the Bagua over it. Having this information before the consultation enables us to begin our conversation about step two - evaluating their needs and life goals—and how to enhance the Bagua areas in their home to achieve them.

In Feng Shui, the ideal floor plan is a rectangle with all four corners falling inside the Bagua. However, most Western homes are not designed this way. Many have cutouts and areas that are missing when overlaid with the Bagua. These areas outside the Bagua can create a void in one's life unless they are corrected or anchored. How to anchor missing areas in the Bagua is discussed in Chapter 6. The following are a few examples of typical floor plans.

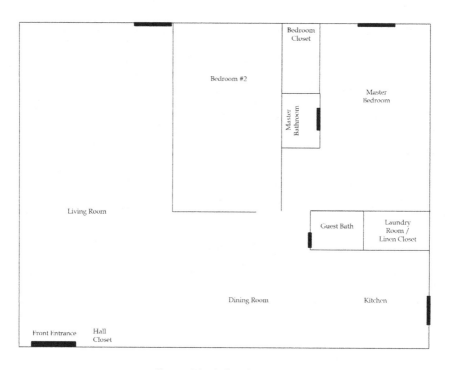

Figure 1 A basic first-floor layout

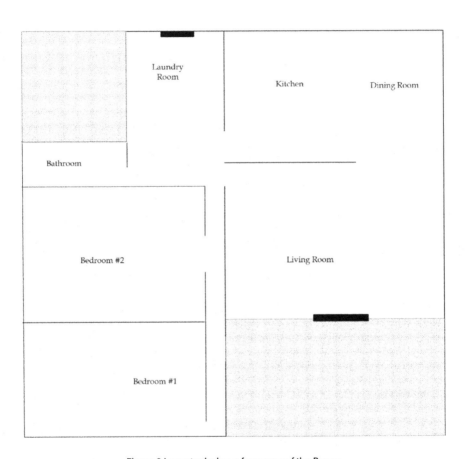

Figure 2 Layout missing a few areas of the Bagua

Figure 3 Layout of an L-shaped home

First floor

Second floor

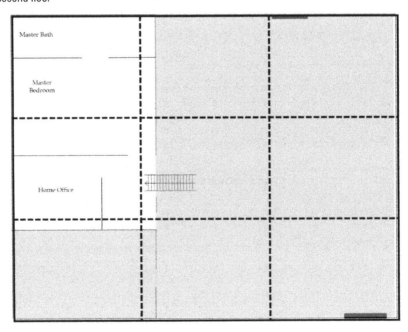

Figure 4 Layout of a two-story home

To begin step one, find an architectural drawing of your home's floor plan or sketch one out yourself.

With a ruler and marker, draw a horizontal line across the bottom of the floor plan to connect the farthest outside walls of the front of your house. Include decks and attached garages. Next, draw a line across the top. This line indicates the back of your house.

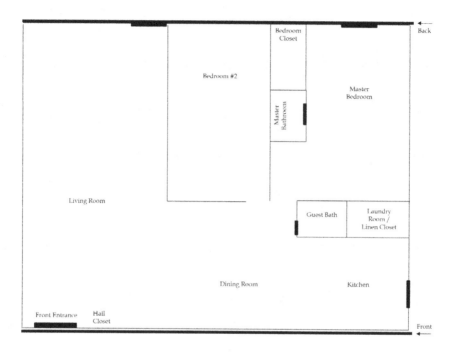

Figure 5 Drawing the first and second Bagua lines on a basic first-floor layout

Next, draw a vertical line to connect the farthest outside walls of the right side of your house, including decks and attached garages. Draw another vertical line to connect the farthest outside walls of the left side of your house. Include decks and attached garages.

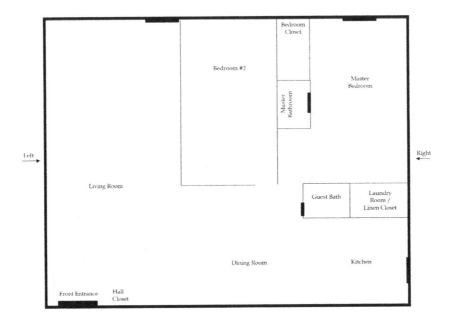

Figure 6 Drawing the third and fourth Bagua lines on a basic first-floor layout

Finally, measure the horizontal and vertical lines and divide them into thirds. Draw dotted lines at the one-third marks between the horizontal and vertical lines to create a nine-square grid. If you find that some areas of the Bagua are missing or outside the house or apartment structure, shade in those areas for now.

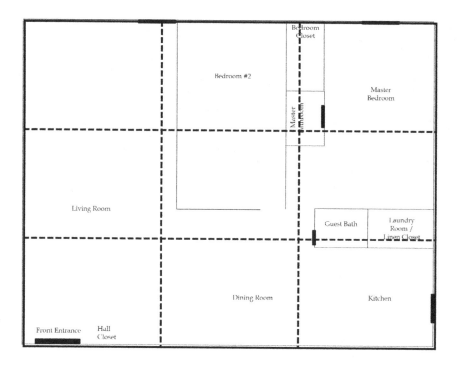

Figure 7 Drawing the grid lines on a basic first-floor layout

If you have multiple stories, create a Bagua for each floor. If your second floor is open, such as a loft or a home with a cathedral ceiling, and only covers a portion of the main floor, shade in the areas that are missing in the Bagua (see Figure 8).

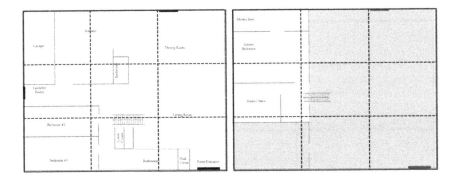

Figure 8 Drawing of two stories

Multiple stories give certain Bagua areas of your home an extra boost. For example, if your Love, Marriage, and Relationships area is downstairs in the dining room but also upstairs in your guest room, you can enhance both areas to bring more love into your life.

When the Bagua grid is superimposed over the floor plan, the home's main entrance is always located at the lower line of the grid (usually in the Knowledge and Self-Cultivation, Career, or Helpful People and Travel areas, although in the case of U-shaped houses, the entrance may be recessed into the Center area). Once you have oriented your Bagua grid to the main entrance of your structure, label each of the nine areas to complete it. I tell my clients that once they map out their home it will begin to tell a story and shed some light on issues they may be facing in their life.

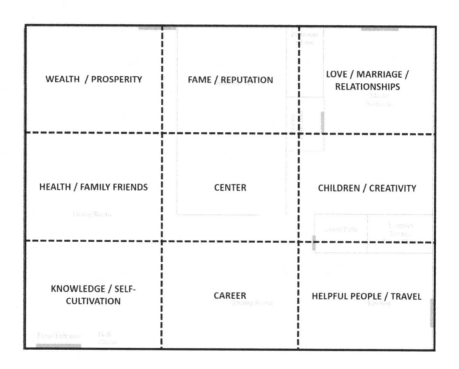

Figure 9 Completed Bagua

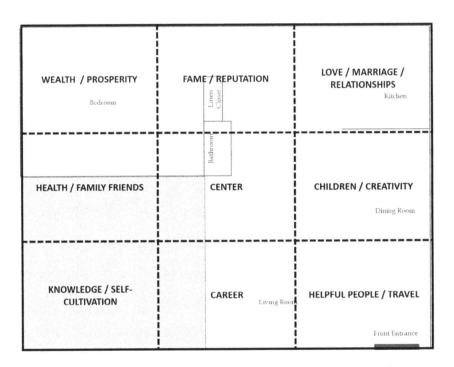

Figure 10 Completed Bagua over layout of an L-shaped home

This home is missing the Knowledge and Self-Cultivation area
and most of the Health, Family, and Friend area.

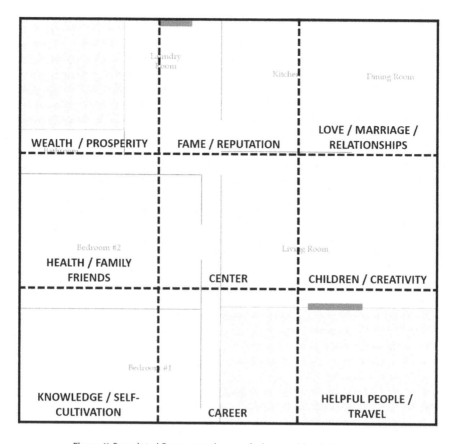

Figure 11 Completed Bagua over layout of a home with missing corners
This home is missing Helpful People and Travel,
most of Wealth and Prosperity, and part of Career.

What Is Your Home Telling You?

Is your garage cluttered? (If it is connected to your house, the garage is part of the Bagua.) Are dirty clothes piled up in your bedroom? Do you have a bed that is not made? Is your guest room used for storage or unfinished projects? Think about where these rooms are in relation to the Bagua map. Is the story of your life unfolding? When looking at a home through Feng Shui eyes, you can usually find trouble spots quickly. Areas that are missing from your map can also provide clues as to what is going on in your life.

Feng Shui at Work

A client of mine was stressed over his romantic relationship. It had stopped working for him, and he was unhappy all the time. A key discovery was that his Love, Marriage, and Relationships area was where he kept his wastebasket and broom. Throughout the day, he would sweep up and leave piles of dirt in that corner, symbolizing a love life swept into the corner and neglected. Another client was having a hard time getting her finances organized. Her cluttered bedroom closet was in her Wealth and Prosperity area. Simple enhancements, such as his disposing of the piles of dirt and moving the broom to a closet, and her decluttering her bedroom closet, made a big difference in their lives. He is in a new loving relationship, and she has found the resources she needs to feel financially secure.

In a thank you note, another client wrote, "I love having these tools to help me be aware of all the aspects of each room. It helps me to focus my energies."

Understanding Each Area of the Bagua

In Your Turn I ask some questions associated with the nine areas of the Bagua map to prompt you to begin thinking about your needs and goals in each area. By answering the questions and completing step one, you will be prepared to evaluate these needs and the goals you want to achieve to address them.

Your Turn

WEALTH PROSPERITY	**FAME REPUTATION**	**LOVE MARRIAGE RELATIONSHIPS**
HEALTH FAMILY FRIENDS	**CENTER GROUNDING**	**CHILDREN CREATIVITY**
KNOWLEDGE SELF-CULTIVATION	**CAREER**	**HELPFUL PEOPLE AND TRAVEL**

↑　　　　　　　↑　　　　　　　↑

ENTRANCE QUADRANT

Career (front center)

How do you feel about your career?

<u>Knowledge and Self-Cultivation</u> (front left corner)

How peaceful is your life?

<u>Health, Family, and Friends</u> (middle left)

How is your health, or that of those around you?

How is your relationship with friends and/or family?

<u>Wealth and Prosperity</u> (back left corner)

How do you feel about your financial well-being?

What else are you prosperous in?

<u>Fame and Reputation</u> (back center)

How are you being recognized at home or at work?

<u>Love, Marriage, and Relationships</u> (back right corner)

How is your relationship with your soul mate?

<u>Children and Creativity</u> (middle right)

How are your children doing?

What are you doing to nourish your creativity?

<u>Helpful People and Travel</u> (front right corner)

Where would you like to travel, and how can you make it possible?

How helpful is your support system?

<u>Center</u>

Do you feel grounded or scattered most of the time?

Chapter 2:
Step 2 - Evaluate Your Needs and Life Goals

If your life is working perfectly, you probably are intuitively already practicing Feng Shui, and Ch'i flows freely throughout your home. If, however, your answers to the questions posed in the last chapter reveal that certain areas of your life are not working well or are causing you stress, applying enhancements to the corresponding areas of your home will allow your environment to support you rather than drag you down.

In addition to asking my client in an initial phone meeting to send me a picture or sketch of the layout of their home so I can lay the Bagua over it, I look up their home's footprint on Google Earth. If the structure is not rectangular, I identify which areas are outside (missing from) the Bagua and will need to be anchored. I also ask them to tell me generally about their life and personal goals.

I then schedule a personal consultation with them in their home. As we sit together in a comfortable space, I ask the following questions:

- What are you hoping to get from this consultation?
- What areas of your life are working?
- What areas are not working?
- What are you hoping to improve?
- What areas of your home do you love the most, and why?
- What areas do you dislike and why?

These are questions you can ask yourself. Write down your answers on the following pages. Reflect on your achievements, joys, stressors, and life goals. Answer each question as honestly and completely as you can. Your answers will give you the information you need to begin steering your life toward realizing your goals. When you have completed this step, you will be ready to analyze your home's Bagua map to prioritize those areas you have the greatest need to improve.

Your Turn

What are you looking for in life?

What areas of your life are working well?

What areas of your life are not working well?

What areas of your life are you hoping to improve?

What areas/rooms in your home do you love the most, and why?

What areas/rooms in your home do you dislike, and why?

Chapter 3:
Step 3 - Analyze Your Home's Bagua – Prioritize Areas of Greatest Need

What is Your Number One Goal?

Now begins the important work: taking your reflections from Chapters 1 and 2 and applying them to the Feng Shui Bagua. Answer each of the questions below with a yes or no. Each number to the right of the question is a subchapter that corresponds to the Bagua area the question addresses.

- Is your career meeting your needs?   _____ 5.1
- Do you have the peace you need in your life?   _____ 5.2
- Are you healthy and thriving?   _____ 5.3
- Do you have a good relationship with family and friends?   _____ 5.3
- Are you financially secure?   _____ 5.4
- Do you have a good reputation?   _____ 5.5
- Is your love life everything you want it to be?   _____ 5.6
- Are your children thriving?   _____ 5.7
- Are your creative juices flowing?   _____ 5.7
- Are you able to travel to places you long to visit?   _____ 5.8
- Do you have a good support network for when you run into trouble?   _____ 5.8
- Is your home helping to keep you grounded and centered?   _____ 5.9

If you answered no to any of these questions, place an X in the corresponding areas on your Bagua map. Go to the subchapters listed below to find the enhancements you'll need to make to these areas in your home:

WEALTH PROSPERITY	FAME REPUTATION	LOVE MARRIAGE RELATIONSHIPS
HEALTH FAMILY FRIENDS	CENTER GROUNDING	CHILDREN CREATIVITY
KNOWLEDGE SELF-CULTIVATION	CAREER	HELPFUL PEOPLE AND TRAVEL

↑   ↑   ↑

ENTRANCE QUADRANT

As you look at the *X*'s marked on your Bagua grid, ask yourself what your home is telling you. Wherever you placed an *X* is where you need to begin your Feng Shui work. You can look at other areas of your home later, but for now, make those areas marked with an *X* your priorities, and pick just one to start. As I tell my students, "You can't do it all at once; therefore, prioritizing is essential." And as another saying goes, "If it ain't broke, don't fix it."

Begin by standing in this Bagua area of your home. What do you see? Is it cluttered, holding items you don't like or that carry uncomfortable memories? Or is the area missing from the Bagua altogether? If the answer is yes, you are ready for step four. It starts with decluttering.

Your Turn

What did you identify as your number one goal?

What area of your home does that goal reside in?

What does that area look like?

Chapter 4:
Step 4 - Clean and Declutter
Areas of Greatest Need

Feng Shui at Work

A client was concerned that her love life was not moving forward; she was lonely and not meeting men. She was also trying to lose weight and had a few large pieces of exercise equipment in her house that were remnants of a past relationship. During a consultation I noticed that the equipment dominated her living room, and one piece was even stored behind her front door, blocking the entrance of Ch'i. She acknowledged that she was not using the equipment and that not only did it clutter her home, it acted as a constant reminder of her past love and the fact that she was not exercising. She decided to pass on the equipment by selling it to someone excited about using it. She used the money she made to buy a membership at a gym where she met her new love. They now exercise regularly together.

Another client felt that she was stagnating in her home environment. Once she made the conscious intention to move forward, she began clearing and giving away items to prepare for the sale of the property. As soon as the space was cleared, she began receiving purchase offers, as well as listings for new properties to look at. She said that "people were coming out of the woodwork." She cleared her energy path and now has found the perfect house with a beautiful view.

How Clutter Affects the Bagua

There is often a correlation between excessive clutter and problems that occur in one's life. For example, a cluttered desk or closet in the Wealth and Prosperity area can lead to feeling stuck with finances. Look at your home with Feng Shui eyes. What are you holding on to that is keeping you stuck?

WEALTH PROSPERITY	FAME REPUTATION	LOVE MARRIAGE RELATIONSHIPS
HEALTH FAMILY FRIENDS	CENTER GROUNDING	CHILDREN CREATIVITY
KNOWLEDGE SELF-CULTIVATION	CAREER	HELPFUL PEOPLE AND TRAVEL

↑   ↑   ↑

ENTRANCE QUADRANT

Decluttering Made Easy

"I can't keep up with my work . . . I go from one fire to another . . . I feel so overwhelmed . . . I don't know where to begin . . . I feel blocked . . . I have no energy . . ." Do you hear yourself or others around you saying such things? Look around. Do you see piles of unfiled papers, items stacked everywhere, blocked doors, overstuffed closets, broken items . . . in other words, *clutter*?

It is time to clear the clutter that is holding you back.

The task does not have to be difficult. You can transform your home from chaos to a comfortable, peaceful haven with the few-minutes-a-day technique I call the "Salami Method of Time Management"—slicing off one piece at a time. Think of eliminating clutter and organizing your possessions as an adventure that will open doors to new opportunities. By getting rid of things you no longer want or need, you will revitalize your home and make room for what you really *do* want to flow into your life, bringing you more happiness, clarity, and peace of mind.

Feng Shui views clutter as a manifestation of two types of chaos: Active chaos and passive chaos. Active chaos is the clutter that results from your creating something, such as while cooking, painting, remodeling, reorganizing, and so on. This clutter will be cleared when the project is completed. Passive chaos is the clutter that stays in piles in closets, under beds, in garages, and generally all over the house. This is the clutter that blocks the flow of the life energizing Ch'i and consequently drains your life. In Feng Shui everything counts, which means that your storage areas are as important as your most lived-in spaces. In other words, if your room is orderly because you have clutter stuffed in your closets, you are not practicing Feng Shui.

Early on in my life I felt a need to organize my belongings. I assigned everything I had an X place to keep it in, and as I was cleaning up, I returned each item to its designated X. An X is a dedicated storage space for each of your items. It could be a drawer, closet, shelf, basket, or plastic storage bin. Retail outlets like The Container Store have numerous solutions for storing things in small, tight places.

To begin decluttering, first pick up the items that are in plain sight and return each to its designated X. Then either donate, toss, or recycle anything you no longer want or need.

Once you have cleared the space of the visible clutter, move to a drawer or a shelf in a closet. Avoid overwhelming yourself and declutter just a little bit every day. For example, if a dresser is the first thing you see as you enter the room, clear the visible clutter from the top of the dresser first. Then move in a counterclockwise direction around the room clearing other areas of visible clutter. On another day, return to the dresser to declutter the top drawer, the next day the second drawer, and so on. Give yourself permission to remove items that you no longer use, are broken, or that hold negative memories. Either pass them on or toss them out.

When I retired from my career in education, I realized I no longer needed all my business clothes. So, I created a "one-third" rule for myself, which meant that if I had nine skirts, I would remove at least three of them. Apply this formula to a sock drawer. If you have eighteen pairs of socks jammed into a drawer so tightly it is difficult to close, allow yourself to remove and pass on at least six pairs. Once you begin using this system, you may find you want to rid yourself of even more than a third of the items you have accumulated.

Decluttering a little bit every day does not take long, and the results are noticeable almost immediately. You will start to feel the positive energy flowing through your home, your personal energy will be renewed, and life-changing opportunities will start coming your way.

Feng Shui at Work

A client hired me because she lacked energy. After a successful home consultation, I received an email from her stating: "Today I went to the hall to get a ladder to continue my enhancements and found that one thing led to another. The task of storing the cleaning products we just bought led to cleaning out the linen closet. I went to my tool drawer for a hammer, saw the air vents were dirty, and began cleaning them. I went to enhance the sewing room and decided to move the piles from the table, and then I looked in the closets and took out clothes to give away. I then thought that since I have cupboards in here, why do I have all this computer stuff out? I rearranged the laptop cords to be stored neatly behind the desk. Before I began, I felt very tired. Now I feel so much better. I have so much energy and enthusiasm." My client's life continues to improve daily.

In her book *The Happiness Project,* Gretchen Rubin shares the joy of having an empty shelf. Imagine the wonderful feeling of having so little clutter that you could reserve a whole shelf for the sheer pleasure of seeing it empty. For Rubin, an empty shelf "means possibility" and "a space to expand." Once you have emptied a shelf by culling items in your closet, for example, you might choose to add a few decorative items related to that Bagua area. My closet is in my Health, Family, and Friends area, so I decided to put a few pictures of my friends on a shelf I had emptied of unused items. I love seeing their happy faces each time I step into the closet. Once you feel the positive results of clearing your space of clutter, you will not want to stop.

Remember that your environment mirrors your consciousness, and there is no more revealing place to see it reflected than behind closet doors.

During transition periods in my life such as retirement, a kitchen remodel, and my mother's passing, I was faced with the challenges of organizing and disposing of items I had acquired as a result of those events. Many of them held loving memories, and I had to ask myself, *What is the best way to let go of things that remind me of my loved ones but that I no longer have use for?*

I decided to give most of them a new lease on life rather than keep them in storage. When I was clearing my closet of excess professional clothing, I donated some to charities and sold some at upscale consignment stores. That was the first step in a process of transformation. I had more room in my closet, others were enjoying the clothes, more Ch'i was free to circulate, and new business began coming my way.

Surveying Mom's items, I thought about who might want them for the memories they evoked. I passed on some of her jewelry, clothing, small memorabilia, art, and furniture to friends and family members who were thrilled to receive them. I sent some of her photo albums to family members who were pictured in them and sold some of her antiques to antique dealers. I felt better about passing these items on, knowing others would enjoy them. As I said earlier, I believe in doing a little at a time. In decluttering your area of greatest need, begin with just a drawer, a shelf, or the top of a cabinet. Baby steps build momentum.

Feng Shui at Work

I was saving an American Girl doll with a trunk filled with clothes for my granddaughter. My daughter was thirty-five at the time and had just had a son. The doll sat unused, and her clothes were fading. I decided to pass her on with love to a friend's seven-year-old grand-daughter. I re-dressed her in a new outfit and felt the doll becoming beautiful again. The little girl loved the doll and clothes so much that she wrote me a beautiful thank you note.

In a second example, our kitchen remodel turned out to be a blessed opportunity to lovingly pass on appliances, cabinets, and countertops to friends and family. My sister-in-law posted pictures of how beautiful our microwave oven looked in her kitchen. We made several people happy while we were enjoying the lightness of our new kitchen. As we began putting things back in the cabinets, we tried to pass on at least a third more of what we had.

In Feng Shui there is a saying: "If you want a change in your life, move or remove twenty-seven items in your home." Why twenty-seven? The numbers three and nine are auspicious numbers in Chinese numerology. The number three represents expansion and eternity, while the number nine represents "triple perfection," or harmony. These numbers symbolize our soul's evolution and the ending of things that no longer serve us. When the energies of these numbers are multiplied together, they equal the number twenty-seven, which symbolizes unconditional love, humanitarianism, harmony, and spiritual insight. My husband and I move or remove twenty-seven items from our home every December to welcome in positive change for the coming year.

Watch for new opportunities coming into this Bagua area of your life because you have let go of the old and made room for the new. Decluttering is the foundation of beginning Feng Shui—clearing the path for positive energy to flow in.

Practice Inner Feng Shui

As you spend time clearing physical items you no longer need, take time to also clear mental clutter. Are there behaviors in your life that make you unhappy? For example, always being late, procrastinating, not getting enough sleep, overeating, putting off exercise, being critical and negative? Unhappiness with your behavior drains your energy. On the other hand, good Feng Shui nourishes it. As you approach making behavioral changes, begin small. Choose one behavior you want to change and write a positive affirmation for the result you want to achieve. For example, if you are always late, your affirmation might be, "I make sure to leave enough extra time when I go somewhere to ensure that I am on time." Focus on this behavior, elicit the help of friends, and reward yourself for small accomplishments.

As you let go of negative behaviors, replace them with behaviors that are positive and transformational:

- Show gratitude
- Meditate
- Breathe deeply
- Listen to music
- Laugh it off
- Exercise
- Spend time with friends
- Help others

Affirmations

In Feng Shui, intention plays a valuable role in enhancing any area of your home or business, as do affirmations that strengthen the potential of any result you want to manifest. Therefore, every enhancement should be made with clear intent. Written or stated affirmations expressed as if the result has already happened are powerful. Affirmations reinforce the assumption that your words and thoughts will become a reality. Examples of affirmations to make while you are clearing your home of clutter are:

- "Wonderful new opportunities have just come my way."
- "Our home is alive with positive energy, peace, and harmony."

Feng Shui on a Shoestring

Passing on items from your home and letting go of negative behaviors costs nothing but leads to huge payoffs. When I visit my mom's friends, I bring something of hers for them to remember her by. They love the memories, and I know that the items are going to good homes.

Now that you've decluttered your area of greatest need, you are ready to move to step five to start making enhancements that will draw in the Ch'i and help you to achieve your goals.

Your Turn

What is your plan for decluttering your area of greatest need? What can you pass on, and to whom?

What can you do to take care of your inner Feng Shui?

Write an affirmation to begin your decluttering work.

Chapter 5:
Step 5 - Ch'i Enhancers to Help You Achieve Your Goals

Enhancing the Nine Bagua Areas

May of my clients have asked if Feng Shui is all about hanging mirrors and crystals. I tell them not to worry; there are numerous options for enhancing one's space. These options are called Ch'i enhancers. Ch'i enhancers are the basic Feng Shui tools used for treating, stabilizing, and balancing the energy in your environment. The ten Ch'i enhancers taught by the Western School of Feng Shui[TM1] are:

1. **Art**: paintings, sculptures, collages, collections, and textiles
2. **Colors**: hues associated with each Bagua area
3. **Crystals**: round and faceted to circulate Ch'i
4. **Lighting**: electrical, candles, oil, natural light
5. **Living things**: plants, flowers, animals
6. **Mirrors**: the bigger the better except for in bedrooms and dining rooms*
7. **Objects of nature**: rocks, shells, seeds, potpourri
8. **Sound makers**: wind chimes, bells, musical instruments
9. **Whirligigs**: mobiles, flags
10. **Water features**: fountains, ponds, birdbaths, aquariums

*Mirrors create active energy which is too much for both bedrooms and dining rooms where the energy needs to be peaceful and calm.

Art and Colors

Of all the Ch'i enhancers, I have found that art and colors are the easiest mediums for lifting the energy in a Bagua area because of their powerful effect

---

1   From course materials, Western School of Feng Shui™. All Rights Reserved.

on personal energy. According to Feng Shui, our homes should be nurturing places for us mentally, physically, and spiritually. To accomplish this, we need to ensure that our surroundings accurately reflect who we are as individuals and who we aspire to become. Feng Shui is about finding the personal Ch'i enhancers that not only match the Bagua area we are enhancing but also reflect our personality and style.

Art is the soul of a room; it gives it energy and life. Feng Shui makes it easy to place your art in the Bagua areas that will act to enhance your life and bring you closer to your goals. Here are some examples.

- In Career: Enhance with waterscapes or art that represents moving water or your careers goals
- In Knowledge and Self-Cultivation: Enhance with serene, wooded landscapes or representations of spiritual guides
- In Health, Family, and Friends: Enhance with floral art or portraits of family members
- In Wealth and Prosperity: Enhance with art in the color purple or that represents opulent scenes
- In Fame and Reputation: Enhance with art in red tones representing celebration or upward movement
- In Love, Marriage, and Relationships: Enhance with romantic art representing couples or pairs of items
- In Children and Creativity: Enhance with whimsical, fun, creative art; portraits of children or pets
- In Helpful People and Travel: Enhance with travel pictures; representations of mountains or spiritual guides
- In Center and Grounding: Enhance with art in earthtones representing the earth; sunflowers, yellow trees, fields

Choose art that makes you happy and does not evoke any negative thoughts or memories. It has been said that "A picture is worth a thousand words." What does your art say to you?

Feng Shui at Work

Years ago, I had two single female clients who were looking for love. Both had decorated their homes beautifully with very interesting art. Unfortunately, both had also placed a large painting representing a lonely singular figure in their respective Love, Marriage, and Relationships areas. One had hung a painting in her dining room of a lonely cowboy with his head lowered. At our consultation I recommended that she replace it with more romantic art, which she did with a beautiful wall hanging of two intertwined hearts. The other had a large painting in her bedroom of a single zebra, also with its head lowered. She replaced it with a picture of two lovers holding hands. Both women have found meaningful relationships since. What you hang on your walls can make a difference in your life!

During a consultation we move art around to best suit the energy of the room. My clients love feeling the shift when art is rearranged to enhance a space. They can feel it!

Subchapters 5.1–5.9 provide ways to apply Ch'i enhancers to each of the Bagua areas in your home.

Your Turn

What is the area of the Bagua that addresses your greatest need and number one goal?

What art enhancers can you use to begin transforming the energy in that area?

Chapter 5.1
Career

CAREER

**With love you can
manifest harmony,
peace, and your capacity
to visualize your life's
purpose to find your
destined path.**

Feng Shui at Work

"Recently, a close relative was floundering in a career blockage. A Feng Shui visit from Maria revealed that many areas in her living space were conflicting with the flow of energy. Moving and/or eliminating some of her decorations had almost immediate effects: she received a deposit payment for future legal services the next day. She had hung a career vision board in the space, and one week later the job offer she had hoped for was received! Wow."

The testimonial above was from a satisfied client. I had held the consultation in a small room the client was renting, and the Career area was the wall at the foot of her bed where she had hung a rock 'n' roll poster. Knowing this was the first thing she saw every morning; I advised her to replace the poster with career images on a vision board. She even hung her résumé with the word "Hired" across it. The results were dramatic: she is now a successful attorney. She has continued with Feng Shui consultations and practices at each stage of her career and each residence she has lived in. She now has her own law practice, has recently purchased her first home, and is in a loving relationship.

If enriching your career is your area of greatest need, you have come to the right place for help. Have you been struggling with statements such as these?

- "I have been looking for a rewarding career for a while now and so far... nothing."
- "I don't feel valued in my current job, and my skills are not being utilized."
- "My workplace is chaotic...I never feel as if I can get projects accomplished."

Applying some basic Feng Shui principles to the Career area of your home can help turn these kinds of statements into: "I love my job."

Testimonial:

"Hi Maria!! Oh my goodness things are definitely starting to flow around here. While I'd like to give my husband credit for his hard work, I can't help but connect it to the changes we've made with Feng Shui. He has more than tripled his annual income in the last few months!!! I am in shock really. We haven't even finished our changes either. I just want to thank you so much for all of your expertise and input. This is unreal. He's a believer in the fountain! He checks to make sure it's working all the time now. My husband kept announcing these huge settlements the last few weeks to our family, and my 13-year-old son, who had been making fun of my hanging crystals said, "OK Mom, maybe those crystals do really work!""

WEALTH PROSPERITY	FAME REPUTATION	LOVE MARRIAGE RELATIONSHIPS
HEALTH FAMILY FRIENDS	CENTER GROUNDING	CHILDREN CREATIVITY
KNOWLEDGE SELF-CULTIVATION	CAREER	HELPFUL PEOPLE AND TRAVEL

↑   ↑   ↑

ENTRANCE QUADRANT

The Career area is nestled in the front center of the Bagua, which could be the front entrance to your home or business, or an office, bedroom, kitchen, garage, or front porch. Whatever is located there, making specific Feng Shui enhancements to this area will help you achieve your career goals. In the *I Ching* it is called "deep water" because you need to dive deep within yourself to get in touch with what you really want in life.

By enhancing the Career area of the Bagua, you will help renewed energy lead you to making positive changes in a current job, advancing to a more successful career, seeking volunteer or community service opportunities, pursuing meaningful activities in your retirement, or just exploring your life's purpose. In other words, finding a more satisfying, conscious, and creative path for yourself.

The Element for Career

The element for the Career area is Water. It can be represented inside and outside your home or business in mirrors, glass, and cut crystal; flowing asymmetrical shapes or wavy lines; the black and dark tones in the color spectrum; art depicting water; and water features such as aquariums, fountains, and birdbaths. (Water from fountains should always flow toward the house and birdbaths must always be kept clean.)

If your Career area is your front entrance, make sure that when you open the door you are greeted with a clean and inviting space. Then bring in the Water element to encourage the flow of Career energy.

Interior Enhancements for the Career Area of Your Home or Business

(Choose One or More)

- Begin by decluttering the space.
- Install art depicting moving water (such as streams, ponds, rivers, or oceans). This is a great location for a small fountain or aquarium.
- Add decorator items or furniture in black or very dark colors or having asymmetrical shapes.
- Hang or place mirrors and/or display glass/or crystal items, such as a crystal vase or a glass table. A round faceted crystal hanging from the ceiling helps the energy flow in small, confined spaces.
- Display career images and symbols (books or logos from your business or those you aspire to), if your space allows it. A vision board, as described in Chapter 7, can be a useful addition here to help you realize your goals.
- At the entry of my home, which is in the Career area of the Bagua, I hung a large mirror on one side of the door that reflects my father's painting of the Mediterranean Sea. I also placed a small fountain on a glass table with a glass holder for my husband's and my business cards.

Figure 12 Mirror and wall hangings with asymmetrical shapes represent the Water element

When I was in the classroom, the Career area is where I taught my lessons with a screen, whiteboard, projector, and so on. I also hung posters of waterscapes, filled the bookcase with career-oriented books, and added a small fountain. My daughter's Career area was in her kitchen, where she placed a beautiful ocean scene and hung a crystal in the window. Additionally, she placed a small fountain on the counter. After working as a successful assistant executive director of an office in the California State University system, she started her own management business and already has a lucrative contract.

Dark colors, art representing moving water, asymmetrical shapes, mirrors and other glass items, and career images are all Feng Shui Career enhancements no matter where the Career area in your home is located, even if it is a hallway.

Feng Shui at Work

> A client was retiring and was searching for his true calling as a consultant. After I met with him, he painted his front door a deep burgundy, placed fountains on either side of the door, and hung a large mirror on one side of the entrance facing a seascape on the other side. He wrote affirmations describing perfect consulting opportunities. Success! He retired and is now making more money through his new consulting business than when he was working at his prior job. Feng Shui works!

Exterior Enhancements if Your Career Area is also the Front Entrance of Your Home or Business (Choose One or More)

- Ensure that your front walk is clutter free and that there are no dead or dying plants visible.
- Activate the Water element by installing a water feature, such as a fountain with water flowing toward the house, to keep the energy flowing inward, or install a 360-degree bubbling fountain close by. A fountain with the water flowing away from the house symbolizes the Ch'i flowing out. This is also a good place for a small pond if it is kept clean and circulating.
- Use wind chimes to invite the Ch'i to enter, plant colorful healthy flowers along the path (curved if possible) to your door, and place two greeters in the form of plants or statuary on either side of the door. An easy fix is to replace an old welcome mat with a new, vibrant one.
- Regardless of which Bagua area it falls in, the front door is especially important in Feng Shui. Therefore, anything you can do to emphasize and beautify it will encourage new opportunities to come your way. Painting the door a shade of red will not only draw attention to your home but also, according to Chinese cultural thought, invite prosperity and positive energy into it. If red doors don't appeal to you, pick a color that delights and inspires you, and keep it clean and fresh. Also, clean and maintain any front-door lighting, or install some if needed.

Figure 13 360-degree bubbling fountain

What to Avoid in the Career Area

- Too many earth tones (they represent the Earth element which dams Water)
- Items stored behind doors that hinder them from opening all the way
- Piles of stuff and overall clutter that make it easy for the Ch'i to get stuck

Feng Shui at Work

A client recently moved into an apartment. She owns her own business and was having trouble finding a suitable workspace. I advised her to strengthen the Career area of her home. Typical of apartment complexes, each door looked alike, so she placed two large black, shiny pots on either side of her front door with tall red plants. This created a striking entrance, allowing the Ch'i to find her. Inside, she hung a mirror and art representing ocean waves flowing inward and placed her affirmations in a glass bowl. Since implementing these changes, she successfully located a beautiful new workspace that she moved into within a month. Her business has taken off!

Another client was stuck in an unsatisfying career. She realized that she had been neglecting the dying plants by her front door. Her house was telling her to remove the dying plants, replace them with colorful flowers, and hang a beautiful plant in a red metal holder. Her energy increased as did her career opportunities. She took a job at another firm, received a promotion, and is thriving. Small changes can make a big difference.

A Career Area Not Located Within the Bagua

If your Career area is "missing" from your floor plan, I recommend anchoring the space with a fountain, wind chimes, red and yellow flowers, greeting statues, or hanging plants to invite the Ch'i's attention. The key is to complete the space with attractive objects that create a welcoming environment. (Anchoring missing areas is discussed in detail in Chapter 6.)

Sample Affirmations for the Career Area

- "I love my career."
- "I feel fulfilled in the work that I do."
- "I attract many positive opportunities and circumstances to share my talents."

Feng Shui on a Shoestring

Just the act of hanging an inexpensive wind chime by your front door calls in the Ch'i to nourish your life. Planting or displaying fresh flowers and decluttering the area also start the energy flowing, and affirmations are free.

If Career is your area of greatest need, making a few simple changes in your home can have an immediate and powerful effect. Be prepared to have doors of opportunity open for you—perhaps even opportunities completely different from any you expected. You could be very pleasantly surprised! Enjoy the flow of renewed energy which will lead you to achieving your goals.

Your Turn

How do you feel about your career? What is missing? What would an ideal career look and feel like to you if you were achieving your goals?

Find your Career area on the Bagua. What room is located there? How is it decorated? Describe it in detail: colors, elements, decorations, art. Is it in good condition? If it is outside the structure, what is there now?

Does this area contain things that are broken, messy, or out of place? Clear the area of these items first for a quick win.

Make a note of the items in this area that are nurturing your career. Make another note of the items that are hindering it.

What can you do with the items that are hindering your career? Clean and repair them? Give them away? Move them to a more appropriate room?

List the enhancements you want to make to this area. Check them off as you complete them!

Bless your new space and write your affirmations below. You can also place your affirmations in this area or simply state them as you are enhancing it.

Be open and ready to experience wonderful new career opportunities as you achieve your goals.

Once you have made changes in this area, describe any shifts you notice in your life.

Chapter 5.2
Knowledge and Self-Cultivation

KNOWLEDGE AND SELF-CULTIVATION

Love enters my home, bringing with it grace and guidance. In stillness I will be open to knowing myself; what to say, what to do, where to go.

Feng Shui at Work

A client was a nursing student, studying for an important exam. She was stressed because she could not study and focus on her work at the same time. She was having trouble retaining information and told me her mind felt cluttered. During the consultation we walked into the Knowledge and Self-Cultivation area of her home, and immediately the reason became evident. It was an unused guestroom that had been relegated to storage. Fortunately, it was already a sage green, appropriate for the area. I advised decluttering, removing her schoolbooks and other items she no longer needed. As she did this, she began to regain her energy and focus. I advised bringing in a wooden bookcase to display her most current and important nursing books. She bought a green floral bedspread and pillows and hung a picture of the Tree of Knowledge above the bed. She even found an old picture of Florence Nightingale to display. She brought in some plants and a small fountain. The room was large enough for a wicker chair that she began to use for studying. Across from the chair she hung a vision board with representations of succeeding as a nurse. Guess what? She passed her test with flying colors and soon after began her nursing career at a local hospital.

A client who was missing the Knowledge and Self-Cultivation area decided to anchor it in her garden with two wooden Adirondack chairs facing a statue of Saint Francis surrounded by a round flower garden. It was perfect for stillness. She meditates there and has since located meditation classes to attend.

Even if your Knowledge and Self-Cultivation area is outside the Bagua, as one client discovered, you can anchor it as she did on her patio with a beautiful wicker loveseat, chairs, and a table. She created a perfect area for reading, reflection, and entertaining.

Figure 14 Client anchored her Knowledge and Self-Cultivation area
with a statue of Saint Francis, wooden railroad ties, and chairs.

The Knowledge and Self-Cultivation area is located in the front left corner of
your home or business. Sometimes it will also be outside the structure or in an
attached garage.

WEALTH PROSPERITY	**FAME REPUTATION**	**LOVE MARRIAGE RELATIONSHIPS**
HEALTH FAMILY FRIENDS	**CENTER GROUNDING**	**CHILDREN CREATIVITY**
KNOWLEDGE SELF-CULTIVATION	**CAREER**	**HELPFUL PEOPLE AND TRAVEL**

↑   ↑   ↑

ENTRANCE QUADRANT

Although all areas of your home should lend themselves to harmony, this section of the Bagua is particularly related to "stillness." When you spend time being still and calming your mind, you are better equipped to absorb knowledge and develop insight. In the *I Ching*, the Knowledge and Self-Cultivation area is called "still mountain." Taking time in stillness to cultivate understanding will benefit your entire being.

"*No one can see their reflection in running water, but only in still water.*"
—Taoist Proverb

Does your home nurture a calm and peaceful feeling in you? Do you have a beautiful area in which you can sit quietly in stillness? Or are you surrounded by frenetic energy from the moment you come through the door?

There are myriad things in life that create stress; your home should not be one of them. The serenity you create in your home has a great deal of influence on your outlook.

Testimonial:

> "Soon, as I implemented change and enhanced the energy in my home, I began to view "house" as a metaphor for self. "Keep your house in order" was the refrain that kept running through my mind . . . my spiritual house, mental, physical, and emotional. Within one week there were hummingbirds at my front window, within three I was asked to write website copy, join two women in a retreat business, and was gifted with a monetary benefit to care for my father."

How do you achieve balance and fuel yourself? Where do you go to have quiet downtime? Assess your lifestyle. In our hurried Western society, we pride ourselves on how much we get done in a day. Multitasking has become the thing to do. I am a personal example of this as I even wrote a "how to" guide on the best methods for mastering "multitasking." While multitasking is often a necessity, taking time out to relax, unwind, and rejuvenate is a necessity as well. By learning how your environment affects your ability to balance work, rest, and play, you can make the easy changes that will help you to achieve and sustain that balance and quiet down.

In whatever room your Knowledge and Self-Cultivation area is located, applying some basic Feng Shui principles can help you create a peaceful sanctuary.

By enhancing this area of the Bagua, you will help energy lead you to improving your studies or signing up for classes, training, and workshops that contribute to life enrichment. Enhancing this area is also beneficial if you are on a self-help journey or just want more peace in your life.

The Elements for Knowledge and Self-Cultivation

The elements for the Knowledge and Self-Cultivation area are Wood and Water, since water nourishes wood. While each of the Bagua areas represents one of the elements, the corners of the Bagua will reflect a team of cojoining elements working together in harmony. Wood can be represented in anything made of wood or plants (including fabric and paper); representations of flowers, trees, or plants of any kind; columnar shapes and stripes; the color black; and any shade in the blue or green color spectrum. Because Water nourishes Wood (see the Nourishing Cycle of the Elements in Chapter 8), adding any of the Water enhancements described in Chapter 5.1 will enrich the Wood element.

Interior Enhancements for the Knowledge and Self-Cultivation Area of Your Home or Business (Choose One or More)

- Begin by decluttering the space.
- Enhance with the colors blue, green, or black (representing the Water element) and in the shape of columns and stripes.
- Add art representing still, wooded meditation gardens or calm water scenes.
- Display busts, statues, or pictures of spiritual guides.
- Use wooden furniture and accessories wherever you can and add healthy plants with rounded soft leaves to create a peaceful meditative area.

Exterior Enhancements for the Knowledge and Self-Cultivation Area (Choose One or More)

- Showcase lush plants and trees.
- Create a seating area with wooden or wicker furniture and green or blue cushions for quiet reflection. This is a great place to accentuate with a fountain containing water that flows toward the house.
- Display statues of spiritual guides and blue or green gazing balls.

Note: If this area is where your front door is located, create a peaceful, serene entrance that will invite in the Ch'i.

What to Avoid in the Knowledge and Self-Cultivation Area

- Art that represents the Fire element (red tones), which is very active. Anything white or metal, representing the Metal element which cuts wood.

A Knowledge and Self-Cultivation Area Not Located Within the Bagua

- See Chapter 6 for details on how best to anchor this area using some of the specific enhancements listed above.

Sample Affirmations for the Knowledge and Self-Cultivation Area

- "I feel calm and can think clearly when dealing with stressful situations."
- " I am nourished by the peacefulness of my home."
- "Yahoo! I just passed my exam!"

Ideally, the Knowledge and Self-Cultivation area is where you would begin making enhancements for stillness. But what if your master bedroom, bathroom, or garage is located in this area? Here are some ideas for enhancing these spaces for stillness and calm.

How to Begin the Calming Process

If you find that you are surrounded by chaos, begin small. Look at the area, which may be inside or outside the house, with the intention of creating a sanctuary. Declutter and enhance the area with soothing colors, art, pictures, flowers, music, and objects that you love. Create a five-element display as described in Chapter 8.

Find a small bit of time daily, or at least a few times per week, for "being present" in this space. Breathe, read, meditate, sleep—anything that calms the body.

Master Bedroom in the Knowledge and Self-Cultivation Area

This is a room for rest, health, vitality, and loving relationships. Because sleep has a direct effect on our health and longevity, special attention needs to be paid to calming and beautifying this space. Enhance it with:

- Warm wall colors. Master bedroom walls should be the color of natural human skin tones to create a feeling of warmth. Avoid blue, green, white or grey for walls, which are too cool for a romantic boudoir. Accentuate with plants and wooden furniture.
- Accents in the red spectrum and pairs of items representing romance
- Soft bedding, a chair for quiet reading, soft lighting
- All of these bring in the qualities of the Love, Marriage and Relationship area.

What to Avoid in the Master Bedroom

- Exercise equipment
- Desk and computer
- TVs (can be closed in an armoire or covered with a cloth at night)
- Large mirrors
- These items all activate energy, detract from a soothing calmness, and rob you of sleep and vitality.

Feng Shui at Work

In my home, part of the Knowledge and Self-Cultivation area is outside the house, while the rest is in my master bedroom. To anchor it, I placed a blue-green glass gazing ball outside the missing corner. I also planted a flower garden to enhance the space outside the bedroom window. Having the master bedroom in the Knowledge and Self-Cultivation area was a challenge because blues and greens are too cool for a bedroom (not enough Fire). Ideal colors for bedroom walls are the entire spectrum of skin tones from light cream to dark browns. I had the challenge of bringing in the cool Wood element while keeping the fiery passion of the bedroom. To enhance the serenity of the Knowledge and Self-Cultivation area, I brought in many wood pieces and kept the lights dim. My favorite meditative spot in the house is a brown wicker chair and ottoman in the corner of the room. This is where I love to sit, read, and "be still." I brought in more of the Wood element through a large silk Ficus tree and a few floral arrangements. The walls are a light tan. To maintain the Fire element needed in the bedroom, I hung romantic pictures, included pairs of items such as the two Georgia O'Keeffe poppies over the bed, candles, and figurines, and added accents of burgundy. (More about bedrooms in the Love, Marriage, and Relationships area in Subchapter 5.6.)

Figure 15 Pairs of items in master bedroom

Dining Room in the Knowledge and Self-Cultivation Area

No matter how small the space, the dining room is where we stop to take in nourishment and allow ourselves to peacefully digest. Even if you dine alone, take time to lay out a place setting. Avoid grabbing a quick bite in front of the TV on a regular basis. Enhance the space by surrounding yourself with:

- Candles and soft music
- Decorations in blues and greens
- Art representing calm wooded scenes

Having decorative items you love to look at will enhance taking time to eat slowly and enjoying the moment.

What to Avoid in the Dining Room

- Clutter on the table
- Uncomfortable chairs
- Large mirrors

These things all work to activate energy and will "talk" at you during the entire meal.

Feng Shui at Work

Two clients have found their personal pools of calm. One single woman lays a pretty place setting for her breakfast each morning and looks out at her water view while reading the paper and journaling for a few minutes before starting her day. Another relaxes in her garden hammock with her book for a few minutes after work to decompress before beginning dinner. Peaceful routines like these make a world of difference in well-being.

Bathroom in the Knowledge and Self-Cultivation Area

This room is where you cleanse your body, eliminate waste, and revitalize yourself. It should be a pleasant space to relax in a luxurious bath or shower and be surrounded by:

- Calm art and colors in blue and green shades
- Items that represent the Knowledge and Self-Cultivation area
- Art representing plants that will help calm you as you dress and prepare for the day

What to Avoid in the Bathroom

- Keeping the toilet lid open when not in use. There is a Feng Shui saying: "Where the eye goes the Ch'i flows."

Feng Shui at Work

A client has a small bathroom in her Knowledge and Self-Cultivation area. She has enhanced it with soft shades of greens, silk plants, and decorative wooden items. To make it her calming sanctuary, she placed a Buddha statue with a sand Zen Garden and inspirational words on small rocks, along with inspirational books, on a small wooden table in the corner. It has become a lovely pool of calm in her already beautiful apartment.

Two of my clients have the Knowledge and Self-Cultivation area in their bathroom. One painted a large mural of bamboo shoots on the wall, and the other enhanced her spacious bathroom with the color sage green, a shower curtain with brocade leaves, a picture of a forest, an orchid, a wicker basket of inspirational books, and small wooden figurines. Both areas are calm and soothing.

Figure 16 Whimsical bamboo mural in Knowledge and Self-Cultivation corner of a bathroom

Garage in the Knowledge and Self-Cultivation Area

Many people have their garage in the Knowledge and Self-Cultivation area. Consider the garage a room in your house and enhance it accordingly. Declutter and place items on wooden shelves if possible. Hang art representing peaceful wooded or water scenes. Paint shelves or create accent walls in blues and greens. You can even hang curtains in front of shelves in the same colors. I always recommend hanging a 50 millimeter round faceted glass crystal in the center of the garage to keep the energy flowing. The garage should be a space that makes you feel good as you drive into it.

What to Avoid in the Garage

- Making it a storage area for junk

By regularly practicing Feng Shui, you eventually will turn your entire home into a calming environment. Create the time and space to regularly go inside yourself and be still. A calm and tranquil mind and heart will maintain your vitality and longevity.

Feng Shui on a Shoestring

For not a great deal of money, you can place a small plant, a blue or green vase, or a picture of trees you might already have in your home in your Knowledge and Self-Cultivation area.

Your Turn

Describe your ability to learn and find peace and stillness in your life. What is missing? What would a peaceful life look and feel like to you?

Find your Knowledge and Self-Cultivation area on the Bagua. What room is located there? How is it decorated? Describe it in detail: colors, elements, decorations, art. Is it in good condition? If it is outside the structure, what is there now?

Does this area contain items that are broken, messy, or out of place? Clear the area of these items first for a quick win.

Make a note of the items in this area that are nurturing your ability to be at peace and self-cultivate. Make another note of the items that are hindering it.

What can you do with the items that are hindering your ability to be at peace and self-cultivate? Clean and repair them? Give them away? Move them to a more appropriate room?

List the enhancements you want to make to this area. Check them off as you complete them!

Bless your new space and write your affirmations below. You can also place your affirmations in this area or simply state them as you are enhancing it.

Be open and ready to experience intellectual and spiritual growth and peace in your life!

Once you have made changes in this area, describe any shifts you notice in your life.

Chapter 5.3
Health, Family, and Friends

HEALTH, FAMILY AND FRIENDS

With love, our health and relationships with family and friends are solid, vibrant, and joyful. Our roots connect us and make us stronger.

Feng Shui at Work

A student in one of my classes was concerned about health issues and her lack of energy. Once she applied the Bagua to her home, she discovered that her Health, Family, and Friends area was in her master bedroom closet. She was horrified to discover that her cluttered, messy closet was keeping her from achieving the vibrant health she desperately needed. She began a cleaning and decluttering regimen, donated many items (giving them new life), and allowed herself the luxury of reserving an empty shelf for "possibility." She placed a lovely bouquet of silk flowers on the shelf, hung a green 30 millimeter round faceted glass crystal from the ceiling, and pasted a floral wallpaper strip around the top of the closet. As she worked, she stated positive affirmations. She loves the change her efforts have made; she nourishes herself each time she steps into her closet. While decluttering, she found renewed energy and is now walking daily, eating better, feeling much healthier, and planning to nurture other areas of her home.

Another client had her Health, Family, and Friends area in her garage. Each time she drove in, the first thing she saw was her hot water heater, furnace, and cat box. This was draining her energy daily. I recommended placing a bamboo screen in front of the hot water heater and furnace, attaching posters of healthy flowers and medicinal herbs to it, moving the cat box out of the Health, Family, and Friends area and closer to the front of the garage in the Knowledge and Self-Cultivation area, and replacing it with a covered box draped in a blue cloth. She also placed a large flowering orchid on the workbench. Additionally, she decluttered the garage. Now when she drives in, her energy is nourished rather than drained. I see her at the gym on a regular basis, and she looks great.

The Health, Family, and Friends area is located in the middle left side of your home or business.

WEALTH PROSPERITY	FAME REPUTATION	LOVE MARRIAGE RELATIONSHIPS
HEALTH FAMILY FRIENDS	CENTER GROUNDING	CHILDREN CREATIVITY
KNOWLEDGE SELF-CULTIVATION	CAREER	HELPFUL PEOPLE AND TRAVEL

↑ ↑ ↑

ENTRANCE QUADRANT

If your area of greatest need is health, yours or that of a loved one or family member, or if your relationships need to be rekindled, begin here.

Believe it or not, the energy in your home can help you achieve your health and relationship goals. The Health, Family, and Friends area is particularly associated with "strength and good health." The healthier we are, the more options we have to enjoy life.

Feng Shui seeks to balance energies within a space to promote happiness, health, and good fortune. All of us can benefit from creating a beautiful and aesthetically pleasing environment within our homes—and this can help with health!

The premise of the Health, Family, and Friends area of the Bagua in Feng Shui is the importance of nurturing your physical health and loving family and friend relationships so that you have supportive foundations when unforeseen difficulties occur. In the *I Ching*, the Health, Family, and Friends area of your home or business is called "shocking thunder," as it refers to the many life challenges which may present themselves at any time. The healthier our relationships are with family and friends, the more we prosper from the opportunities and emotional support they provide.

I recently read a quote that sums up the power of Feng Shui:

"You cannot prevent the birds of sorrow from flying over your head, but you can prevent them from building nests in your hair." —Chinese Proverb

Testimonial:

"My physical place feels much more like a cozy and warm home now, like a loving nest that supports me and enhances all my projects."

Whatever room your Health, Family, and Friends area resides in, basic Feng Shui principles can help you nurture and strengthen your health and your relationships.

The Element for Health, Family, and Friends

The element for the Health, Family, and Friends area is Wood. Representations of this element are in the blue and green color spectrums and in columnar shapes or stripes.

All representations of the Wood element are important here: Plants (live or silk), wooden furniture and decorative items, fountains, art representing flowering plants, representations of family and friends. The main difference between representations of the Wood element in the Knowledge and Self-Cultivation and Health, Family, and Friends areas is that while the Knowledge and Self-Cultivation area is best represented by images of peaceful mountains, wooded scenes, and spiritual guides, floral scenes and vibrant flowers best represent the Health, Family, and Friends area. The Knowledge and Self-Cultivation area is more focused on the spiritual plane, while the Health, Family, and Friends area focuses more on the physical.

Are you feeling as vibrant as you would like? Flowers can help! Flowers play an important role in Feng Shui. Their strong colors, beauty, and life can draw powerful Ch'i into your home. Fresh flowers are ideal, but artificial flowers work if they are kept clean and fresh looking.

Flowers also have great healing powers. For centuries they have been used for medicinal purposes, but in Feng Shui, the simple act of surrounding yourself with flowers and placing them in auspicious areas of your home can improve your health and increase your energy. Flowers are living, breathing entities offering us the balance of nature. When healthy and beautiful, they can energize you.

Figure 17 Uplifting flower arrangement

Interior Enhancements for the Health, Family, and Friends Area of Your Home or Business (Choose One or More)

- Begin by decluttering the space.
- Use any shade of blue or green and some watery colors, then add florals.
- For a boost in health, choose to decorate with floral art, floral cloths, floral designs in carpets, or floral wallpaper.
- Bring in plants and fresh flowers, either in flowering plants or cut flower arrangements.
- Enhance with wooden furniture and items made of wood or grass, such as basketry.
- For a boost in relationships, hang pictures of friends and family in this area in black or wooden frames. Create a gallery of joyous pictures of people in healthy, happy states.
- Add your affirmations calling in health and happy relationships.

Exterior Enhancements for the Health, Family, and Friends Area (Choose One or More)

- Make sure the area is clutter free and that there are no dead or dying plants.
- Enhance with lush, healthy flowering plants.
- If you have a window in this area, enhance the view as much as possible.

What to Avoid in the Health, Family, and Friends Area

- The colors white or gray (they represent the Metal element which cuts Wood)
- An excess of circular shapes and anything made of metal
- Art or pictures representing single or sad and lonely looking people

A Health, Family, and Friends Area
Not Located Within the Bagua

- If your Health, Family, and Friends area is missing from your floor plan, you can anchor the area by choosing one or a combination of the cures discussed in Chapter 6.

Sample Affirmations for the Health, Family, and Friends Area

- "I am healthy and thriving."
- "My family supports me in everything I do."
- "I enjoy supportive relationships with loving friends."

Feng Shui at Work

In my home, the Health, Family, and Friends area is in the bedroom foyer and the walk-in closet. We decluttered the closet and removed excess clothing. In the foyer, I placed a glass table with a green runner below a large mirror. The wallpaper consists of lush bamboo and flowers. On the table I have pictures of family and friends displayed in wooden frames and small floral photo albums. It has become a shrine to family and friends.

Special Health Concerns

If someone in your home is having health challenges and is going through or recovering from surgery, activating the energy in the Health, Family, and Friends area of your home is especially important. You can do this easily by:

- Decluttering the area
- Bringing in a healthy flowering plant or a vibrant bouquet of flowers (fresh or artificial)
- Displaying pictures of the person in a healthy, active state in athletic activities or exhibiting health and joy

- Placing blue or green candles in an altar with your pictures and flowers
- Writing or stating affirmations of the positive outcome

If you have a two-story home, enhance the Health, Family, and Friends area of both floors. For a more powerful cure, place flowers in the Health, Family, and Friends area of every room.

Figure 18 Vision board and fresh flowers to activate
energy for good health prior to a medical exam

Feng Shui at Work

A client who was to undergo abdominal surgery had the Health, Family, and Friends area in her bathroom. She hung a picture of a beautiful flower with a hummingbird (the representation of joy) and a collage of family pictures. The room was painted a lovely sage green with a floral shower curtain. I instructed her to always keep drains and the toilet lid closed to keep the vital Ch'i from escaping. Since the bathroom is very small, she hung a round faceted crystal from the ceiling in the center of the room, and placed a small, live flowering plant on the windowsill. She also added written positive affirmations. Her surgery went very well. She has recovered fully and is now working with a personal trainer.

Feng Shui on a Shoestring

Simply moving family and friends' pictures into the Health, Family, and Friends area begins automatically to send energy to you and to those you love.

Clearing this area of dead or diseased plants will halt negative energy from coming into your life. Add just one beautiful, healthy, blooming plant to your Health, Family, and Friends area, make your affirmations, and watch the shift occur.

If this is your area of greatest need, the time is right to enlist the energy in your environment to help you achieve your goals, to strengthen your personal health and the health of those around you, and to build strong, lifelong relationships with your support system of family and friends.

Your Turn

Describe your health, the health of your family members, and your relationship with your friends and family. What is lacking? What would ideal health and/or your relationships with family and friends look and feel like to you?

Find your Health, Family, and Friends area on the Bagua. What room is located there? How is it decorated? Describe it in detail: colors, elements, decorations, art. Is it in good condition? If it is outside the structure, what is there now?

Does this area contain items that are broken, messy, or out of place? Clear the area of these items first for a quick win.

Make a note of the items in this area that are nurturing your health and your relationships with family and friends. Make another note of the items that are hindering them.

What can you do with the items that are hindering your health and your relationships with family and friends? Clean and repair them? Give them away? Move them to a more appropriate room?

List the enhancements you want to make to this area. Check them off as you complete them!

Bless your new space and write your affirmations below. You can also place your affirmations in this area or simply state them as you are enhancing it.

Be open and ready to experience better health and strong relationships with family and friends!

Once you have made changes in this area, describe any shifts you notice in your life.

Chapter 5.4
Wealth and Prosperity

WEALTH AND
PROSPERITY

Abundance and
blessings overflow
with gratitude, giving,
and receiving.

Feng Shui at Work

> A client had her **Wealth and Prosperity** area in her bedroom closet. Fortunately, she was a very neat person, and the closet was orderly. I suggested she remove more items of clothing to symbolically indicate that she was ready for change and hang a purple 30 millimeter round faceted crystal from the closet ceiling to keep the energy moving. Because she was searching for a job in family law, I recommended she frame pictures of families and law offices using a shade of purple matting and hang them with her affirmations inside and outside the closet. Soon after making her enhancements, she received a check for $1,500 that she had been waiting on for quite a while. She now has a rewarding job as an attorney in a family law office.

"Any person who contributes to prosperity will prosper in turn."
—Earl Nightingale

In the Feng Shui Bagua, the Wealth and Prosperity area is located in the back left corner of your home or business. Sometimes it is outside the Bagua grid.

WEALTH PROSPERITY	FAME REPUTATION	LOVE MARRIAGE RELATIONSHIPS
HEALTH FAMILY FRIENDS	CENTER GROUNDING	CHILDREN CREATIVITY
KNOWLEDGE SELF-CULTIVATION	CAREER	HELPFUL PEOPLE AND TRAVEL

↑ ↑ ↑

ENTRANCE QUADRANT

Prosperity does not refer solely to financial wealth. It also encompasses the richness of your life. Are you rich in friends, family, love, community, health, talent, career, self-fulfillment, inner peace and/or finances? How prosperous are you? You can easily take positive steps to contribute to your own prosperity—and Feng Shui can help. If in Chapters 2 and 3 you identified Wealth and Prosperity as your area of greatest need, this is where you begin.

Feng Shui utilizes your positive connection with your environment to help clear the way for blessings to enter your life.

In the *I Ching*, the Wealth and Prosperity area of your home or business is called "persistent wind." It is not about winning the lottery or hitting it rich in the stock market but about steadily gathering resources to secure present and future happiness on all fronts.

Begin your prosperity work by culling and organizing the old to make way for the flow of new abundance. Take time to look at your home's Wealth and Prosperity area and ask yourself, *"Is the area enhancing or draining my prosperity? What can I do to improve this area of my life?"*

Testimonial:

"We put everything into practice as best we could, and it has really worked! Every day I am energized at work, everyone has been super helpful and collaborative, and things are definitely opening up opportunity wise! Also, for my mom's house, we put the house on the market at 7:00 pm on Weds 1/6, and 2 days later, we had 15 showings this weekend, and 2 offers in already! This Feng Shui really works! We can't believe it."

The Elements for Wealth and Prosperity

The elements for the Wealth and Prosperity area are Fire and Wood. The Fire element is represented in any shade of red, ranging from pink tones to burgundy and purple; cone and triangle shapes; any type of lighting; anything derived from animals; art representing people, animals, suns, stars. Adding representations of the Wood element, such as plants or items made of wood, helps to nurture the Fire enhancements. And because Water feeds Wood, incorporating all three elements further encourages the flow of Ch'i. Picture a beautiful fountain surrounded by purple plants near a wooden table with a deep burgundy or red umbrella.

Interior Enhancements for the Wealth and Prosperity Area of Your Home or Business (Choose One or More)

- Begin by decluttering the space.
- Add any shade of purple, red, or blue, which evokes the feeling of richness.
- Enhance with vibrant live or artificial plants having rounded leaves.

- Install water features such as fountains, waterfalls, or aquariums. Water will feed the Wood element, which in turn feeds the Fire element. Prosperity flows in with water both in the Wealth and Prosperity and Career areas.
- Display art in the colors purple, red, or dark blue, that represent wealth, or depict large family gatherings.
- Display valuable possessions.
- Add affirmations calling in prosperity.

Exterior Enhancements for the Wealth and Prosperity Area (Choose One or More)

- Continue enhancing with the colors purple, red, and blue in flowers, pots, cushions, umbrellas.
- Add a water feature flowing toward the home or business. (Waterfalls or 360-degree bubbling fountains work well here in letting prosperity flow.)
- Call in the Ch'i by adding flags, whirligigs, mobiles, or wind chimes.

What to Avoid in the Wealth and Prosperity Area

- Anything old, worn, and in poor condition
- Clutter of any form, which blocks prosperity from flowing

A Wealth and Prosperity Area Not Located Within the Bagua

If your Wealth and Prosperity area is missing from your floor plan, you can anchor the area by implementing one or a combination of the ideas recommended in Chapter 6.

Sample Affirmations for the Wealth and Prosperity Area

- "I feel very comfortable with my finances."
- "I have an abundance of blessings through my family and friends."
- "I just signed a lucrative book deal."

Feng Shui at Work

A recent client has the Wealth and Prosperity area in her dining room. She chose to paint the walls a shade of purple and add purple accents to her table setting. She replaced a large mirror which was too active a feature for restful dining with an opulent painting of beautiful blooming flowers. She also placed two up light table lamps and a few opulent items on the sideboard. She soon had the opportunity to reconnect with family members she hadn't seen in a long time. She became aware of how prosperous she was in family relations. Feng Shui works in mysterious ways!

Figure 19 An opulent purple dining room with gold table setting

Feng Shui at Work

Friends of mine have a lovely L-shaped home with a large lawn area in the missing Wealth and Prosperity area. They chose to enhance and anchor the area by planting a beautiful walking garden to include that exact corner, with a large angel statue sitting on top of a mound near purple flowers, gazing balls, and a cozy bench for sitting and reflecting on all the riches in their life. Their family prosperity has been greatly enhanced with two beautiful grandchildren and various opportunities to travel and reconnect with family and old friends. These are true blessings!

Our own home had two offenders. We were missing our Wealth and Prosperity corner, and to make matters worse, the bathroom was adjacent to the missing corner. We created a "structural" anchoring by building a wooden arbor connecting the existing deck to the missing corner. We planted a red and purple trumpet vine to climb the arbor, symbolizing the upward growth and blooming of prosperity, and planted a deep burgundy ornamental cherry tree nearby. We hung a purple and orange fish windsock at the top of the missing corner and have a deep purple gazing ball at the base. All our outside flowers in this area are in the purple spectrum. We enhanced the bathroom by hanging a large Georgia O'Keeffe print of purple petunias and hung a lavender 30 mm round faceted glass crystal in the corner near a lavender orchid. This has helped our serenity and finances immensely.

Figure 20 Sage green walls; asymmetrical wood-framed mirror in Health, Family, and Friends area extending to a missing Wealth and Prosperity area

Figure 21 Purple flowers facing missing Wealth and Prosperity
area in Health, Family, and Friends bathroom

It is especially important to enhance a bathroom that is in your Wealth and Prosperity area. Remember that all drains and toilet lids must be kept closed when not in use, to keep prosperity from flowing down the drain. Ch'i flows very much like water and tends to be pulled down an open drain, especially an opening as big as a toilet bowl.

Feng Shui on a Shoestring

Shopping in your own home is when you move art and items you already own to a more auspicious location in your home. Find art with purple tones to place in your Wealth and Prosperity area.

This is a great time to remove dead plants and replace them with inexpensive cell packs of annuals. A client told me she planted purple flowers in her Wealth and Prosperity area and received a check she was waiting for in an even larger amount than she was expecting. Focusing on positivity and the prosperity of family, friends, and love is free.

Your Turn

How do you feel about your prosperity? What is missing? What would ideal prosperity look and feel like to you?

Find your Wealth and Prosperity area on the Bagua. What room is located there? How is it decorated? Describe this area in detail: colors, elements, decorations, art. Is it in good condition? If it is outside the structure, what is there now?

Does this area contain things that are broken, messy, or out of place? Clear the area of these items first for a quick win.

Make a note of the items in this area that are nurturing your prosperity. Make another note of the items that are hindering it.

What can you do with the items that are hindering your prosperity? Clean and repair them? Give them away? Move them to a more appropriate room?

List the enhancements you want to make to this area. Check them off as you complete them!

Bless your new space and write your affirmations below. You can also place your affirmations in this area or simply state them as you are enhancing it.

Be open and ready to experience more prosperity in your life!

Once you have made changes in this area, describe any shifts you notice in your life.

Chapter 5.5
Fame and Reputation

FAME AND
REPUTATION

With love, we strive for
integrity and enlightenment.
Our abilities and skills are
acknowledged, respected,
and rewarded.

Feng Shui at Work

A client was renting a room in a house, had just passed the bar exam, and was looking for a position in a law firm. Her Fame and Reputation area happened to be above her bed. I recommended a vibrant picture in reds of two birds in flight representing upward movement. Directly across from her bed was her Career area, so I had her place her diploma and awards there, along with images of the law firms she was considering applying to. She also placed her affirmations in each of these areas. She soon got a lucrative job in a prominent law firm and a new apartment. I later went to help her enhance her new office, and we turned the wall behind her desk into a Fame and Reputation wall with all her recognitions of accomplishment. She became so highly regarded in the legal community that she started her own law firm. She is now experiencing a successful career.

In the Feng Shui Bagua, the Fame and Reputation area is located in the back center of your home or business.

WEALTH PROSPERITY	**FAME REPUTATION**	**LOVE MARRIAGE RELATIONSHIPS**
HEALTH FAMILY FRIENDS	**CENTER GROUNDING**	**CHILDREN CREATIVITY**
KNOWLEDGE SELF-CULTIVATION	**CAREER**	**HELPFUL PEOPLE AND TRAVEL**

↑   ↑   ↑

ENTRANCE QUADRANT

"I feel invisible at work." "No one asks for my opinion anymore." "How can I get more positive recognition?"

There is a saying: "If I take care of my character, my reputation will take care of me."

What you put out will come back to you.

It has been fun for me to see my work in Feng Shui come to fruition. Many of my clients recommend my services to others, and that tells me that my reputation is preceding me. It energizes me to hear that a client seeks me out because they see how their friend's life has changed for the better after a consultation.

In the *I Ching*, the Fame and Reputation area of your home or business is called "clinging fire." A negative reputation creates distance between you, your friends, and coworkers and jeopardizes your happiness. As the *I Ching* states, it "clings" to you. Therefore, you always want to be conscious of building a good reputation that your friends and coworkers will respect and trust.

If this is one of your areas of greatest need, begin at the back center area of your home and evaluate what you see going on there. If it is cluttered and not attractive to you, apply any of the following recommendations to begin reenergizing the space to your benefit.

The Element for Fame and Reputation

The element for the Fame and Reputation area is Fire, represented by anything in the red color spectrum, ranging from pink tones to burgundy and purple. Red is one of the most powerful colors in Chinese culture. It represents fame, fortune, joy, festivity, longevity, and protection from bad luck. The entire back of your home or business which encompasses the Wealth and Prosperity; Fame and Reputation; and Love, Marriage, and Relationship Bagua areas benefits from representations of the Fire element. The difference in the kinds of representations of Fire to enhance with is in the different shades along the red color spectrum and the type of energy you want to create. For the Fame area, the shade is vibrant red. For Wealth and Prosperity, it is shades of red, blue, or purple. And for Love, Marriage, and Relationships, it is shades of red, pink, and white. Adding representations of the Wood element, such as plants or items made of wood, helps to nurture your Fire enhancements.

The Fire element is also represented in the shapes of cones and triangles, and any type of lighting; anything derived from animals; art depicting people, animals, suns, stars. Representations of the Fire element can be used inside and outside your home or business.

Interior Enhancements for the Fame and Reputation Area of Your Home or Business (Choose One or More)

- Begin by decluttering the space.
- Add shades of vibrant red, which bring power to fame and reputation.
- Enhance the area with personal images of fame, such as your rewards, diplomas, certificates, trophies, and any other acknowledgments of achievement.
- Display art in shades of red, images signifying upward movement and celebration, stars, suns, people, animals, and vision boards portraying images of your future goals.
- Add items in the shape of cones or triangles.
- Implement all forms of lighting, including natural light, candles, twinkling, solar, and electrical.
- Add your affirmations calling in a good reputation.

Exterior Enhancements for the Fame and Reputation Area (Choose One or More)

- Continue enhancing with the red color spectrum in flowers, pots, cushions, umbrellas.
- Decorate with representations of suns, stars.
- Add uplighting and twinkle lights.
- Install a fire pit and/or barbecue grill.
- Add your affirmations calling in a good reputation.

What to Avoid in the Fame and Reputation Area

- Paintings or art that represent water
- Too much of the color black, representing the Water element which douses fire
- Any Water element, such as fountains, waterfalls, or pools

A Fame and Reputation Area Not Located Within the Bagua (as in a "U-Shaped" Home)

If your Fame and Reputation area is missing from your floor plan, as in a U-shaped home, you can anchor the area by applying one or a combination of the cures described in Chapter 6.

Sample Affirmations for the Fame and Reputation Area

- "People seek me out for my good reputation at work."
- "I have many friends who ask for my advice."
- "My family looks up to me."

Figure 22 Art representing celebration in Fame and
Reputation area in red and purple tones

Feng Shui at Work

In Feng Shui, if you want to add more energy to a specific area of your life, you can apply the Bagua to that specific area in the same way you apply it to the entire floor plan of your home. Stand at the entrance of the room you want to enhance and imagine the Bagua laid over it. In our home office, we enhanced the wall that fell within the Fame and Reputation area of the room by hanging awards, certificates, and recognition photos. Half the wall is for my husband's acknowledgments of achievement and the other half is for mine. These documents are framed in wood to further feed the Fire element. Spending time in this room is a boost to our self-esteem.

Small changes can make a big difference, both positive and negative. When you find that you are struggling, it is important to recognize when some changes you make produce the wrong effect. I had colorful paintings of dancing ladies on my Fame and Reputation wall. During that time, everything was going great at work. On a whim, I found some beautiful burgundy, green, and gold wall hangings and decided to replace the celebrating, dancing ladies with those. Almost immediately, I felt the shift. My new boss changed existing procedures and meeting structures, and I was no longer involved in higher-level meetings. I felt slighted and unimportant. I consulted with one of my Feng Shui teachers and identified the problem. Although beautiful, the new wall hangings had vertical asymmetrical shapes representing Water instead of Fire. I decided to move them to my Career area foyer alongside a large mirror, because Water is the element that supports Career. The dancing ladies returned to the Fame and Reputation wall, and I was able to retire with recognition. I went on to start this wonderful consulting business.

Figure 23 Fame and Reputation wall in office

Feng Shui at Work

My daughter's Fame and Reputation area was out on her patio. She had struggled with finding a job where she was appreciated and able to learn and grow. Together we went shopping and found three large stars that she hung on the fence. She also cleared the area of garbage cans and bikes, placed a large barbecue grill under the stars, and added a wicker seating arrangement with red cushions. Shortly after making these enhancements, her reputation earned her a position as director of a fast-growing company where her skills were both utilized and appreciated. She has since become an assistant executive director, dabbled in real estate, purchased several homes, and started her own management business.

It is especially important to enhance a bathroom that is in your Fame and Reputation area. Remember that all drains and toilet lids must be kept closed when not in use to keep fame from "flowing down the drain." Using any of the enhancements listed above, you can turn your bathroom into a beautiful shrine to your fame and reputation.

Feng Shui on a Shoestring

Go shopping in your own home to find items that can be moved to enhance your Fame and Reputation area. Select art that includes vibrant red tones and depicts celebration and upward movement. Look for places you can display awards and certificates that you or family members have earned.

Remember that you build your personal reputation through everything you do, whether in big actions or small, and that Feng Shui can help you create an energizing environment that will help your fame and reputation grow.

Testimonial:

"The effects of Feng Shui on my business have been incredible. From the time we did the consultation and the actual corrections, we experienced positive results. From that moment forward the flood gates opened. This year has been unbelievably successful. Our financial success has blossomed. Another benefit . . . people often make comments about how good it feels to be in my shop."

Your Turn

How do you view your reputation, either at work or with your friends and family? What is missing? What would fame and an ideal reputation look and feel like to you?

Find your Fame and Reputation area on the Bagua. What room is located there? How is it decorated? Describe it in detail: colors, elements, decorations, art. Is it in good condition? If it is outside the structure, what is there now?

Does this area contain items that are broken, messy, or out of place? Clear the area of these items first for a quick win.

Make a note of the items in this area that are nurturing your fame and reputation. Make another note of the items that are hindering them.

What can you do with the items that are hindering your fame and reputation? Clean and repair them? Give them away? Move them to a more appropriate room?

List the enhancements you want to make to this area. Check them off as you complete them!

Bless your new space and write your affirmations below. You can also place your affirmations in this area or simply state them as you are enhancing it.

Be open and ready to experience more fame and a reputation to be proud of!

Once you have made changes in this area, describe any shifts you notice in your life.

Chapter 5.6
Love, Marriage, and Relationships

LOVE, MARRIAGE, AND RELATIONSHIPS

Create a loving relationship with yourself or with another, joining two hearts together as one.

Many of my clients ask me the same questions: "How can I find love? How can I strengthen and reenergize the romance in my life?" I answer them by explaining the connection between the quality of their home environment and the quality of their relationships, and that enhancing the energy in their home can help them achieve their loving relationship goals.

If in Chapters 2 and 3 you identified finding love as your area of greatest need, begin by focusing on the Love, Marriage, and Relationships area of the Bagua, which is in the back right corner of your home or business.

WEALTH PROSPERITY	FAME REPUTATION	LOVE MARRIAGE RELATIONSHIPS
HEALTH FAMILY FRIENDS	CENTER GROUNDING	CHILDREN CREATIVITY
KNOWLEDGE SELF-CULTIVATION	CAREER	HELPFUL PEOPLE AND TRAVEL

↑   ↑   ↑

ENTRANCE QUADRANT

Feng Shui at Work

"I can't seem to find romance that lasts. Since I moved into this house, my relationships begin, but then just seem to poop out. I want a meaningful relationship to last. I want to be someone's Valentine. What can I do?" This was the request from one of my recent clients. I had my suspicions, and as we began the consultation, her house told the story. Her Love, Marriage, and Relationships area was situated in a sunroom in the back corner of the house. It had become a storage room for everything left over from her move. It was cluttered and, unfortunately, also the location of a messy cat box.

I encouraged this client to declutter the sunroom immediately. She organized the storage boxes into "giveaways," "throwaways," and "keep." Next, she painted the room a soft mauve and added white wooden bookcases to feature books and romantic items, including a pair of red candles, two lovebirds, and a pink flower arrangement. She found a few posters of couples in different romantic locations (hugging under the Eiffel Tower and strolling hand in hand on a beach), which she hung in wooden frames. She found a wonderful white cat box structure with a roof and draped a dish towel with red hearts over it to further enhance it. It looked like a piece of furniture. She made affirmations and stepped back to enjoy the lovely room. She called me to share the good news of the wonderful new relationship she was in and that "this one's a keeper."

In the *I Ching*, the Love, Marriage, and Relationships area of your home or business is called "receptive earth." This means beginning with loving yourself and being receptive to the give-and-take of a relationship with your soul mate.

One of the best ways to honor and love yourself is to give yourself the gift of a warm, well-balanced, and decluttered home. When you take time to give yourself little gifts, it becomes much easier to receive them from other people.

Many of my clients just want to enjoy their single life and loving themselves. All the Feng Shui enhancements for love still apply. Remembering the connection between romantic love and self-love, treat yourself lovingly every day. Use your best bedding, wear your best nightclothes, light candles, buy yourself flowers. To attract love, be completely loving with yourself.

In whichever room of your home this area of the Bagua resides, using basic Feng Shui principles to enhance it can help you nurture and strengthen yourself and your relationships, and even send out energy to help you find your perfect soul mate.

The Element for Love, Marriage, and Relationships

The element for the Love, Marriage, and Relationships area is Fire which is represented by any shade in the red color spectrum, from pink tones to burgundy and purple, along with white (the color of the Metal element); the shapes of cones and triangles; any type of lighting; anything derived from animals; and art depicting people, animals, suns, stars. Representations of the Fire and Metal elements can be used inside and outside your home or business.

Because the Wood element feeds fire, adding representations of wood, such as plants or items made of wood, help to nurture your enhancements. Think of a beautiful red or pink orchid with two stems representing romance.

Figure 24 Enhanced Love, Marriage, and Relationships corner

Interior Enhancements for the Love, Marriage, and Relationships Area of Your Home or Business (Choose One or More)

- Begin by decluttering the space.
- Add shades of red, pink, and white.
- Enhance with art representing pairs (lovebirds, two hearts, two candles, etc.) and romantic themes.
- If you are already in a relationship, display pictures of you and your significant other.
- Display items in the shapes of cones or triangles, or representations of hearts.
- Add your affirmations calling in love and romance.

Exterior Enhancements for the Love, Marriage, and Relationships Area (Choose One or More)

- Continue with the red, pink, and white color spectrum in flowers, pots, cushions, umbrellas.
- Display garden art in pairs.
- If you have room, add a bistro table with two chairs.
- Add your affirmations calling in love and romance.

What to Avoid in the Love, Marriage, and Relationships Area

- Art that represents single people or evokes emotions of sadness or loneliness
- White, gray, blue, or green wall colors in the master bedroom. These are too cool for romance.
- Too much of the color black, representing the Water element which douses fire

A Love, Marriage, and Relationships Area Not Located Within the Bagua

If your Love, Marriage, and Relationships area is missing from your floor plan, as in a cut-out corner, you can anchor the area by applying one or a combination of the cures listed in Chapter 6.

Sample Affirmations for the Love, Marriage, and Relationships Area

- "I am my own best friend."
- "I love life and feel loved in return."
- "I am in a romantic relationship with my soul mate."

Feng Shui at Work

Two of my clients had their Love, Marriage, and Relationships area outside the Bagua, and both anchored this missing corner outside their homes with cute red seating arrangements. One added a white bistro table and two red chairs, accenting with a flowering pink azalea on the tabletop. She soon got into a romantic relationship and is now happily married. The other placed two red camp chairs under a tree. She told me that just after making this small enhancement with her intention, she noticed that men were beginning to speak to her more. Doors have opened for her, though she found herself relishing her single life and is doing a lot of traveling and enjoying time with her grandchildren. Both are great examples of how Feng Shui enhancements can lead to both romantic love and self-love.

Figure 25 A client anchored her missing Love, Marriage, and Relationships corner with this bistro table and chairs.

The Master Bedroom

In Feng Shui, the perfect room for the Love, Marriage, and Relationships area is the master bedroom. Unfortunately, not all homes are designed this way and rooms other than the master bedroom may occupy the back right corner of your home. No matter where on the Bagua map your master bedroom is located, it is still considered the most important room for Love, Marriage, and Relationships. If your master bedroom is in another Bagua area, you will want to enhance it with the elements that represent that area, as well as with the elements that represent Love, Marriage, and Relationships. As you decorate, declutter, and enhance this area, it is important to incorporate some of the red spectrum colors to bring in the Fire element, along with pairs of items and romantic representations.

If you are single and looking for a relationship, you should design the room as if two people are already living there. For example, make sure there are two nightstands, two lamps, and extra room in the closet. This signifies the intention that you want to share your life with another person. I even suggested to one of my clients that she hang two lush burgundy robes in the adjacent bathroom.

Wall colors in the master bedroom should be any of the natural skin tones, from light cream, pinks, and peaches to warm reds and dark browns. The room should evoke feelings of warmth, coziness, and romance. Blues, greens, whites, gray, and black are too cool for bedroom walls.

Confusing the Love, Marriage, and Relationships Area with the Children and Creativity or Health, Family, and Friends Areas

- Avoid filling the master bedroom with stuffed animals, dolls, or other relics from childhood.
- Also, avoid displaying pictures of your children and family here. This sometimes catches clients off guard because in Western cultures, many master bedrooms become extensions of family rooms. However, if you want to spark love and romance in your relationship, this area needs to be dedicated to you and your significant other only. This is your place to love and nurture yourselves and each other. Save the pictures of your family and children for your Children and Creativity and Health, Family, and Friends areas. Focus on making this space a romantic boudoir.

Feng Shui at Work

One of my clients was in an unhappy relationship that was stuck and going nowhere. In our consultation, we focused on her bedroom, which was painted a cool green and featured many pictures of landscapes and water. Nothing signified romance, passion, or warmth. She changed the pictures to romantic art, added candles to the bedside tables, and spruced up the room with red-toned accents. Shortly after, she and her boyfriend broke up. This may sound like a bad thing, but Feng Shui works at giving you what you need to live your best life, not necessarily what you think you want. After getting out of her unhappy relationship, she was free to meet the right man. In her new house, she followed the lessons she learned in our consultation. She now has a wonderful man in her life, and they are expecting their first baby. She could not be happier!

Applying Love, Marriage, and Relationships Enhancements to Other Rooms

No matter which room resides in the Love, Marriage, and Relationships area, you can easily apply the same enhancements, colors, and items that are recommended for the master bedroom. Here are a few examples of applying specific enhancements to other rooms located in this area of your home:

- Kitchen. Enhance with items in shades of red, pink, or white, as in towels and floor mats. Wherever possible, display a picture of yourself with your significant other and keep items in pairs.
- Dining Room. Add a set of romantic salt and pepper shakers, two rose-colored candles in beautiful candlesticks, and/or a picture of yourself with your significant other. Set the table for two and accent in reds, pinks, and/or whites.
- Bathroom. Hang pictures of romantic vacations and add a pair of matching candles or a beautiful flower arrangement in the red color spectrum. Remember that all plumbing needs to be working (no leaks) and drains

and toilets should always remain closed when not in use. You do not want anything to drain your romantic energy.

- <u>Office</u>. Display two paperweights or a picture of yourself with your significant other.
- <u>Children's Rooms</u>. Display pictures of you with your mate, place items in pairs, and display fun art representing pairs.
- <u>Guest Room</u>. Hang art representing pairs, hang inspirational sayings representing romance, display hearts, a red vase with pink or red flowers. You can also bring in red or pink tones with the bedding.
- Remember that the choices are endless. Enjoy discovering them and be creative!

Feng Shui at Work

In my home, the Love, Marriage, and Relationships area is in the kitchen and deck immediately outside the kitchen window. The window ledge above the sink has numerous small pictures of my husband and me in red frames, a set of lovebirds, a few shells we collected on trips together, and a pair of bud vases where I always keep fresh pink or red flowers. Looking out on the deck, I can see a wicker table with red cushions, a red flower arrangement on the table, and a mobile of two red lovebirds. As I cook, I can feel the warmth of our relationship. I consider my husband my best friend!

Figure 26 Romantic representations in kitchen located
in the Love, Marriage, and Relationships area

If creating a healthy loving relationship with yourself and another is a high priority for you, you can further energize your home for romance by enhancing the Love, Marriage, and Relationships corner of every room in your home. Remember to start with the Love, Marriage, and Relationships area and the master bedroom of your home first, then make similar enhancements in every other room. This is especially important if your home is missing the Love, Marriage, and Relationships corner of the Bagua.

To add supplementary enhancements to other rooms, pick a room and stand at the entrance facing in. Locate the back right corner and place one or more of the enhancements mentioned above in the space. For example, consider placing a picture of you and your partner there, or two stems of a red/pink orchid, red/pink candles, a pair of lovebirds, or romantic art.

As I write this, I am looking at a picture located in the Love, Marriage, and Relationships corner of our new office of my husband and me riding our tandem bike. And in the back right corner of my desk, I have a picture of the two of us on a beach. Yes, you can even apply the Bagua to your desk, using where you sit as the Career entrance quadrant. Here is an example of the Bagua applied to my desk: Black chair and black keyboard in Career; notepaper, books, phone, and calendar in Knowledge and Self-Cultivation; silk flower in Health, Family, and Relationships; computer monitor in Wealth and Prosperity; nameplate with silver award star in Fame and Reputation; a picture of my husband and me in Love, Marriage, and Relationships; a picture of my grandchild in Children and Creativity; files in Helpful People and Travel; and a square blotter in the Center.

Figure 27 The Bagua applied to a desk

Feng Shui on a Shoestring

Just the act of writing affirmations and placing them in the back right corner of each room will begin to energize the romance in your life.

Create a space in your home and life for a perfect relationship with yourself, and your perfect mate. Enlist the energy in your environment to help you achieve your goals. Love is coming your way!

Your Turn

Are you in a romantic relationship? Describe it. What is missing? What would an ideal romantic relationship look and feel like to you?

Find your Love, Marriage, and Relationships area on the Bagua. What room is located there? How is it decorated? Describe it in detail: colors, elements, decorations, art. Is it in good condition? If it is outside the structure, what is there now?

Does this area contain items that are broken, messy, or out of place? Clear the area of these items first for a quick win.

Make a note of the items in this area that are nurturing love and relationships. Make another note of the items that are hindering them.

What can you do with the items in this area that are hindering love and relationships? Clean and repair them? Give them away? Move them to a more appropriate room?

List the enhancements you want to make to this area. Check them off as you complete them!

Now look at your master bedroom through the same lens. How is it decorated? What colors and items nurture romance? Which do not? Make the recommended enhancements.

Bless your new space and write your affirmations below. You can also place your affirmations in this area or simply state them as you are enhancing it.

Be open and ready to experience a stronger relationship with yourself, new love in your life, or a strengthened bond with your significant other!

Once you have made changes in this area, describe any shifts you notice in your life.

Chapter 5.7
Children and Creativity

CHILDREN AND CREATIVITY

With love, intuition and creativity are infinite joyous possibilities.

The Children and Creativity area can affect many aspects of your life. It can be enhanced for your children's well-being as well as to express your own personal creativity and whimsy. If your area of greatest need concerns your children (whether they are infants, younger children still living with you, or young adults who have moved out), fertility, or just your creativity and inner child, the following suggestions will help you achieve a calm and creative environment.

This chapter recommends enhancements for the following situations:

- Calming children's rooms
- Creating a welcoming nursery
- Aiding fertility
- Creating a creative space when children move out
- Honoring your inner child
- Creating a space to foster and inspire your own creativity

Feng Shui at Work

I was asked to do a consultation at the home of a couple who wanted to renew their energy. When asked what areas of their home they liked the least, they indicated the bedroom at the right. When we walked through this room located in their Children and Creativity area, I noticed it was being used for storage. On the wall hung a picture of their son who had grown and moved away several years before, and with whom they had become estranged over the years. They missed him and were very sad. The room held lonely memories and was closed off. It was no wonder their energy was low. I recommended decluttering the room, hanging a 30 millimeter round faceted crystal in the center to circulate the energy, installing a small tabletop fountain to further move the energy, and adding more family pictures along with those of their son. My clients loved to sew and do woodworking, although they had stopped doing these activities. I suggested they start using the room to display their crafts. These enhancements helped the couple to focus on clearing and revitalizing the room and to get back to the hobbies they enjoyed. Soon after, they received a phone call from their son and are in the process of reuniting with him.

The Children and Creativity area is in the middle right side of your home or business.

WEALTH PROSPERITY	FAME REPUTATION	LOVE MARRIAGE RELATIONSHIPS
HEALTH FAMILY FRIENDS	CENTER GROUNDING	CHILDREN CREATIVITY
KNOWLEDGE SELF-CULTIVATION	CAREER	HELPFUL PEOPLE AND TRAVEL

↑   ↑   ↑

ENTRANCE QUADRANT

In the *I Ching*, the Children and Creativity area of your home or business is called "joyous lake" because it represents your inner child and your children's well-being.

The Element for Children and Creativity

The element for the Children and Creativity area is Metal. Metal is represented by anything made of metal, the minerals in the earth, rocks, crystals, and precious stones. Its colors are in the white and pastel colors, and its shapes are circles and ovals.

Interior Enhancements for the Children and Creativity Area of Your Home or Business (Choose One or More)

- Begin by decluttering the space.
- Add shades of white and pastels.
- Enhance with art representing children or created by children, as well as fun, whimsical art. This area is a great place for a craft room to exhibit your personal creativity.
- Display pictures of your children, as well as items associated with your childhood.
- Add items made of metal, and items in circular or arched shapes.
- Add your affirmations calling in children's success and creativity, whether theirs or yours.

Exterior Enhancements for the Children and Creativity Area (Choose One or More)

- Continue with the pastel and white color spectrum in flowers, pots, cushions, umbrellas.
- Display metal or whimsical garden art.
- Install a children's play structure, swings, sandbox, or a children's garden. Plant a tree here when a child is born.
- Enhance with a metal seating arrangement, bringing in circular and arched shapes.
- Decorate with natural stones.
- Add your affirmations calling in children's success and creativity, whether theirs or yours.

What to Avoid in the Children and Creativity Area

- Too much of the color red, representing the Fire element which melts metal.
- In children's rooms, avoid a lot of active decorations and colors. Focus more on pastels and calm colors.

A Bathroom in the Children and Creativity Area

My daughter did a beautiful job decorating her baby's nursery (which is in the Helpful People and Travel area). It was a peaceful, harmonious room. She had a dilemma though: both her master bath and guest bath resided in the Children and Creativity area (Jack and Jill style). Bathrooms have a bad reputation in Feng Shui, but they certainly are a necessity! If you take good care of the energy in the bathroom, celebrate it, and make it a beautiful room, it will nurture your energy in turn. Keep it clean and clutter free, and make sure the toilet lid is down and drains are closed when not in use.

Feng Shui at Work

My daughter took these recommendations to heart and transformed both her bathrooms into beautiful, uncluttered, clean rooms holding positive energy. Because there was already a great deal of white with the tub, toilet, and counter, she brought in a soft, sandy buff color with art and wall colors, and added gray towels and shower curtains in a gray and gold print that tied it all together. She enhanced both bathrooms with whimsical art of healthy children at play, hummingbirds representing joy, and pictures of her little boy in metal frames. She added yellow candles, sweet scents, and her affirmations. Her bathrooms became joyous places.

I once was asked by a guest why I have pictures of my grandchildren on every wall in my guest bathroom. I told her it was my Children and Creativity area, and that I wanted to feel their happy, healthy energy each time I used it. Another guest said that I should have a camera in there to record people's reactions when they see pictures of my grandchildren making silly faces. Truly heartwarming!

A Laundry Room in the Children and Creativity Area

Feng Shui at Work

A few years ago, I heard about a woman who was at a loss as to how to enhance her Children and Creativity area because it was her laundry room, which she felt was strictly utilitarian. She did not realize that it was a diamond in the rough. After learning more about Feng Shui, she decided to decorate the room with a collage of all her children and grandchildren. She already had the white metal of the washer and dryer, and she further enhanced the room by adding representations of her loved ones. She is energized each time she does laundry, which she no longer thinks of as a chore. I loved her ideas, and because my laundry room is also in this area, I chose to make large photo collages of my daughter's pictures from birth on, as well as pictures of all my grandchildren. I chose to paint the walls a pastel yellow and added a yellow orchid and whimsical art. I love doing laundry now, and my daughter and grandchildren are thriving.

Figure 28 Collage of children's pictures in a laundry room
located in the Children and Creativity area of the Bagua

133

Children's Rooms—Calm or Chaotic?

Feng Shui is all about creating an environment that radiates positive energy and nurtures your life. This same principle applies to children. Using Feng Shui to enhance a child's bedroom helps to create an environment that fosters happiness and good health, sound sleep, positive and respectful relationships with parents and siblings, and education. Children and parents can enjoy success and healthy relationships if the environment supports them.

Children sleep better in serene environments. Being surrounded by clutter, bright colors, and an excessive number of toys and other stimuli not only affects their behavior but their sleep. Like the master bedroom, this room is designed for rest and nourishment. It's important that the enhancements you choose create a peaceful atmosphere.

Enhancements for Children's Rooms

- <u>Colors</u>. Replace bright primary colors with soft pastels such as lavender, peach, light yellows, mint, softer greens and blues, soft light gray, cocoa, or muted earth tones.

- <u>Art and photos</u>. Change from decorative themes that are too active to a motif that is calm and tranquil. Include inspirational posters and self-esteem boosters. You can also use art and photos in a subtle way to achieve desired results. For example, if your child is a bit unruly, having family photos that include the parents in the room is a subtle Feng Shui solution to calm his or her energy. If your child feels shy, use art with big open horizons, and warm reassuring colors. And, of course it is always a self- esteem builder to use your children's art not only in their room but throughout the house. Pay attention to what your child looks at every day.

- <u>Possessions</u>. Avoid overwhelming children with too many items on display. Rotate a selection of comfort toys and keep the rest out of sight in cabinets and closets. This way when the child tires of the visible toys, the "hidden" ones can be brought out and become new again.

- <u>Electromagnetic frequencies</u>. These are harsh energies emitted by electronic devices that also keep a child from sleeping well. Arrange furniture so that your child's body is two feet away from computer towers, computer monitors, and power strips. Keep them an adult arm's length away from TVs. Cover TVs and computers at night while the child is sleeping or keep them in cabinets that are easily closed.

- <u>Furniture placement</u>. When possible, the bed should be positioned with its headboard against a solid wall. Make sure there is room to walk around each side of the bed. If possible, avoid pushing one side up against the wall or placing it under a window.

- Another rule in Feng Shui is that the foot of the bed should not face the door so that the energy from your body does not flow out the door. If there is no other way to position the bed, you can counter this effect by placing a footboard or bench at the end of it.

- <u>A space for study and accomplishments</u>. Creating a dedicated space, including a desk with a lamp where your child can study, demonstrates to your child the importance you place on education and your child's educational achievement. Put the desk in the power position, facing the door. One focus of Feng Shui is "safety and comfort." Having a back to a door in any room is disempowering, so, whatever you do, don't position the desk so that your child's back is to the door while they are studying.

Welcoming a Baby with a Healthy Nursery

As I was writing this, I was surrounded by the joy of the birth of my third grand-child and babies being born to friends and family members. I watched them all preparing calm, nurturing nests for their new little ones. Getting ready for a new baby requires a lot of planning, and Feng Shui can help. You will want a healthy, balanced room that will grow with your child and fill them with inspiration, excitement, and wonder. A good flow of energy in the baby's room will inevitably lead to a happier, healthier child, while a baby's room with a poor energy flow may contribute to a baby who doesn't sleep well and tends to get sick often. Think of the nursery as a special retreat for relaxation and bonding with your little one, and let it delight all five senses.

Figure 29 Welcoming a new baby

My daughter transformed her home office in the Helpful People and Travel area to a calm, nurturing nursery for her new baby. With soft yellow walls and turquoise accents, she evoked the energy of the Helpful People and Travel area with white accents, pictures of family members who act as mentors, and angel statues.

Figure 30 Nursery in Children and Creativity area

The guidelines for nurseries are like those for a child's room:

- Create a harmony of soft pastel colors.
- Use different sources of light in the nursery at different times of the day and night to help balance the energy.
- Keep your baby's bed away from the door and limit the electrical appliances close to the crib. You do not want the crib too close to the door or in line with it, under a window, or in the middle of the room with no support.
- If there is room, bring in a soft, comfortable chair or rocking chair for those special reading or feeding times.
- When creating a baby's room, connect with your own inner child for creative ideas while your adult self keeps an eye on Feng Shui guidelines for creating a space that is nurturing and calm.

Using Feng Shui to create a tranquil and welcoming room for your baby is about more than decorating. It is about expressing your unconditional love, care, and adoration for them, as well as your continuous support throughout the life you will be sharing together.

A Child's Room or Nursery in Other Areas of the Bagua

A great location for a child's room or nursery is in the Children and Creativity area of your home. But when this is not possible, add elements and enhancements to the Bagua area the nursery falls within, as well as some of the enhancements used specifically for the Children and Creativity area. Always remember to keep the room calm.

Here is a sample of children's room enhancements you can make if your child's room is located in another Bagua area of the home:

- In Career (front center). Calm water scenes, inspirational posters, a round faceted crystal representing the Water element, something representing their name
- In Knowledge and Self-Cultivation (front left corner). Live plants, art depicting wooded areas, mountains, hills, or children playing or reading around trees, pastel green or blue
- In Health, Family, and Friends (middle left). Plants, pastel green or blue, pictures of flowers and family
- In Wealth and Prosperity (back left corner). Plants with rounded leaves, symbols of wealth, pastel lavender
- In Fame and Reputation (back center). Diplomas, awards, and acknowledgments; inspirational posters; pastel shades of red or orange
- In Love, Marriage, and Relationships (back right corner). Pairs of items, pictures of child in parent's loving embrace, pastel shades of red or pink
- In Children and Creativity (middle right). Toys, children's art, art or photographs depicting children, whimsical art, whites and pastels
- In Helpful People and Travel (front right corner). Travel posters, art depicting spiritual guides, or pictures of mentors

- In Center and Grounding. Pastel earth tones and yellows; ceramics; items in the shape of squares and rectangles

You may need to find the balance between activating certain Bagua areas and creating a comfortable, harmonious bedroom for your child. Remember that a comfortable and harmonious bedroom makes for a good night's rest, which makes for a refreshed, healthy child.

Sample Affirmations for a Child's Room or Nursery

- "My baby is strong and thriving."
- "Our children express themselves in positive ways; they excel in every way."
- "We are pregnant with a beautiful, healthy baby."
- "I am so thankful for the healthy baby in my life."

Feng Shui on a Shoestring

It doesn't cost any more to begin preparing the room by decluttering, adding a stuffed animal, a cozy chair, and some pictures of babies along with your affirmations. In doing this, the Ch'i will begin to shift in a positive direction.

Your Turn

If You Have Children:

If you have children, describe them. What is each one like? How do they behave?

Describe your relationship with your children. Are you close? Do you argue? Do you share happy times together?

Look at your child's or children's bedrooms. How are they decorated? Describe them in detail: colors, elements, decorations, art. Are they overly colorful and busy? How could you calm them down?

Find your Children and Creativity area on the Bagua. What room is located there? How is it decorated? Describe it in detail: colors, elements, decorations, art. Is it in good condition? If it is outside the structure, what is there now?

Does this area contain items that are broken, messy, or out of place? Clear the area of these items first for a quick win.

Make a note of the items in this area that are nurturing your children. Make another note of the items that are hindering them.

What can you do with the items that are hindering the nurturing of your children? Clean and repair them? Give them away? Move them to a more appropriate room?

List the enhancements you want to make to this area. Check them off as you complete them!

Bless your new space and write your affirmations below. You can also place your affirmations in this area or simply state them as you are enhancing it.

Be open and ready to experience the joy of watching your children thrive and spending happy times with them.

Once you have made changes in this area, describe any shifts you notice in your life.

Aiding Fertility with Feng Shui

Planning for a baby is an exciting process: creating a space for the new arrival, arranging work schedules, finding day care, joyously notifying family and friends, attending classes, reading books, attending baby showers, and purchasing new supplies. But what if you have difficulty getting pregnant? What if you have been trying for a long time? For some, the process of having a baby can involve numerous trips to the doctor, working with fertility clinics, exploring costly procedures such as in vitro fertilization, or looking into adoption. While continuing your recommended fertility treatment plan, you can also use the power of Feng Shui to create energy forces in your home that can aid fertility.

So, what does Feng Shui have to do with fertility? We know that when our home energy is cluttered, messy, and stuck, we feel the same way.

When trying to get pregnant, begin by activating the life force energy of Ch'i in the Children and Creativity area using the enhancements recommended.

If your child's potential nursery does not fall within the Children and Creativity area of your home, make the same enhancements to any room it falls within as if it did. A client created a gallery of her children's pictures in their stairwell, while I filled my laundry room with baby pictures and a vision board when my daughter was trying to get pregnant. There is no end to the creativity this area can generate.

Other Feng Shui Recommendations to Aid Fertility

- Remove any blocks to your front door, such as overgrown bushes or clutter. The front door is considered the "mouth of Ch'i" and is where all energy enters the home. Make this area clean, auspicious, and beautifully welcoming.
- Avoid clutter in the Children and Creativity area, such as crowded closets or junk rooms. Work at getting these spaces cleaned out to allow new creative (fertility) energy to enter your life.
- If there is a bathroom in this area, make sure bathroom doors and toilet lids are shut. Keep a nice light on in this room.
- Feng Shui in your master bedroom is extremely important when you are trying to conceive. Ideally, the head of the bed should be against a solid wall, and the foot of the bed should not face the door. If this is not possible, adding a headboard, footboard, or bench at the foot of the bed will offer stability and protection. Televisions, computers, mirrors, and exercise equipment should be removed. Rest and romance are the only recommended activities in this room.
- One great technique is to place nine metal frames of children in photos on the right wall of the Children and Creativity area of your home (also the right wall of your bedroom). The number nine in Feng Shui is believed to carry good fortune and represents the culmination of a cycle of events reaching a pinnacle. Photos can be in small frames on a table or in larger ones hung on the wall. Once your child is born, you can replace the photos with those of your baby.
- Finally, ensure that your whole house is clean and free from clutter. Let the Ch'i move through the house without bumping into barriers or blockades such as misplaced objects, boxes, or furniture. Keep the main entrance to the home unobstructed and well lit, lights and equipment in working order, and plants looking healthy and well cared for.

Feng Shui at Work

Vision boards are a powerful way to create affirmations and solid depictions of your aspirations (see Chapter 7). My daughter, who was trying for her second child to no avail hung a collage she had made of pictures of pregnant women, newborn babies, and words and phrases from magazines such as "pregnant," "healthy babies," and "joyous." Her Children and Creativity area happened to be in her family room, where she had created a play area for her toddler. His father, an artist, painted a picture of a baby's hand outstretched to touch his and placed it near the vision board. I, knowing the power of Feng Shui, sent positive energy from afar by placing a similar vision board in the Children and Creativity area of her home, which happened to be my laundry room. She was able to adopt a beautiful baby girl, and soon after got pregnant with a baby boy. She now has three healthy children.

Another client had been trying to conceive for over six months and was about to try in vitro fertilization when she and her husband decided it was time to redecorate the existing nursery and give their two-year-old his own "big boy bed." The crib remained in the nursery as a welcoming gesture to the much-awaited infant. Once the nest was fully in place, it did not take long for my client to happily become pregnant. All is ready for their new addition!

When you are trying to conceive, it is always worth taking a comprehensive approach. You want a welcoming environment for the baby to enter. Fortunately, Feng Shui can help to ensure that your home environment supports all your endeavors to welcome a new child into your family.

Your Turn

If You Want to Have Children:

Find your Children and Creativity area on the Bagua. What room is located there? How is it decorated? Describe it in detail: colors, elements, decorations, art. Is it in good condition If it is outside the structure, what is there now?

Does this area contain items that are broken, messy, or out of place? Clear the area of these items first for a quick win.

Make a note of the items in this area that are nurturing your fertility. Make another note of the items that are hindering it.

What can you do with the items that are hindering your fertility? Clean and repair them? Give them away? Move them to a more appropriate room?

List the enhancements you want to make to this area. Check them off as you complete them!

Bless your new space and write your affirmations below. You can also place your affirmations in this area or simply state them as you are enhancing it.

Be open and ready to experience a beautiful healthy baby coming into your life!

Once you have made changes in this area, describe any shifts you notice in your life.

Children Moved Out? Time to Reenergize Your Home

Have your children grown up, moved away to school, or moved out to start a life of their own? Are you left with an empty room and boxes of their stuff? This transition can feel like a sad time, and yet it can be an opportunity for renewal. If you take this time to organize and clear unused items, you can rejuvenate the space and make way for new opportunities.

You have limitless options for what to do with vacated spaces when your children leave home. If they are off to school and come home regularly, you can reenergize your home by cleaning and enhancing their rooms and creating a welcoming place for them to return to. Or, if they have moved out for good, you can transform the newly freed-up space into something you have always dreamed of, like perhaps a craft room, an office, den, meditation room, or a beautiful guest room? Just remember that in Feng Shui every space counts, so avoid using the room as a storage space filled with neglected items and postponed projects. This would only serve to create more stress in your life, the opposite of what you want. Also, do not just close the door to the room or never go into it, as that would cause the Ch'i to stagnate. Make sure to go in regularly to clean, add and regularly water plants and flowers, and occasionally open windows to let in fresh air. This will keep the energy in the room as active as the other rooms in the house.

I have watched clients transform empty rooms into magical spaces over time. The process does not need to be overwhelming. What works is patience and a bit of time management. You can begin to transform your home from chaos to order with a technique that only requires a few minutes a day. Remember the Salami Method of Time Management, slicing off one piece at a time. For example, start with decluttering the closet one day, the dresser another, one wall the next, and so on. Of course, if you are transforming a child's space after they've moved out, it is best to share your goals with them and get their blessings before you begin. Assure them that you will pass on only those items you both feel comfortable letting go of, and that you will box up the other items to slowly give them back for safekeeping in their new residence. This way, they too can take part in the decluttering process.

Feng Shui at Work

One of my clients had both her daughters graduating in the same year. The first graduated from college, moved out, and got her own apartment, while the second graduated from high school and is attending college. She returns frequently to find her bedroom freshly cleaned, organized, and welcoming. The college graduate had a two-room suite which has slowly been transformed to enhance the Ch'i in the house. Her room was turned into a cozy yet manly den for her father's sports collection and TV, while the second daughter's room is being turned into the mother's Zen room and sanctuary. All rooms in the house have been energized by these transformations, and family relations are stronger than ever.

When my daughter graduated from college and moved farther from home, she left us with many boxes from her early college days. Her new apartment was too small to take in all the boxes at once, and I knew that if she tried to move them all it would add a lot of stress to her life. Therefore, I chose the "Salami Method" of clearing her stuff. Once she was settled, I brought her just one random box each time we drove down to visit. She loved rekindling the memories, threw away or sold many of the items, and found treasures she had forgotten about but were easy to assimilate into her home. Little by little, our house has been cleared of the clutter, and everybody is happy.

Fun in the Home: Honoring Your Inner Child

Even if you do not have children, adventures into creativity can lead you into new friendships, careers, and joyful self-exploration. The Children and Creativity area encourages us to achieve joy and satisfaction through creativity and play. This area helps us to nurture and grow that energizing creative spark that lies within all of us, irrespective of the creative medium we choose. It is an area for fun, hobbies, special interests, and childlike qualities; an area where the whimsical is displayed and celebrated.

Feng Shui at Work

A client and her husband did not have children but enjoyed doing many things together. During the Covid shutdown they discovered that they loved cooking together. Amazingly enough, their beautiful gray and white kitchen was in their Children and Creativity area. They had fun tapping into their mutual culinary creativity and expanding their knowledge and love for each other.

Sample Affirmations for the Children and Creativity Area

- "I can tap into my creativity for solutions to keep my home and business thriving."
- "My children are healthy and thriving."
- "My son's room has been transformed into my reading sanctuary. It nurtures me."
- "I love the energy created in my daughter's childhood room. It's beautiful and I feel closer to her than ever."

Feng Shui on a Shoestring

Simply removing clutter from a child's room by rotating the toys in and out of sight can give a child more of an appreciation for the toys that are displayed.

If you have an empty room, a room in turmoil, or a room you would like to turn into a nursery, begin by placing one object you love in that room. This one act will begin to transform the energy. Further the transformational process by decluttering the space a little bit each day and continuing to add items you love. Soon you'll feel the positive Ch'i flowing throughout the room.

Creating vision boards costs virtually nothing, and you can purchase small, inexpensive metal frames for them at thrift or dollar stores. Intention is free!

The Children and Creativity area can greatly influence the well-being of your family, as well as the creativity that keeps you energized and motivated. It is the most fun area of your home; use it to create a whimsical paradise to keep the Ch'i flowing.

Your Turn

Nurturing Your Creativity:

Do you have an empty room in your home? If so, list some ideas for how you could transform it.

What does creativity mean to you? Where are you most creative? Where are you least creative? What creative outlets are you looking to improve or explore? Are you feeling stuck creatively?

Think about your inner child. What messages does he/she have for you?

Find your Children and Creativity area on the Bagua. What room is located there? How is it decorated? Describe it in detail: colors, elements, decorations, art. Is it in good condition? If it is outside the structure, what is there now?

Does this area contain items that are broken, messy, or out of place? Clear the area of these items first for a quick win.

Make a note of the items in this area that are nurturing your creativity. Make another note of the items that are hindering it.

What can you do with the items that are hindering your creativity? Clean and repair them? Give them away? Move them to a more appropriate room?

List the enhancements you want to make to this area. Check them off as you complete them!

Bless your new space and write your affirmations below. You can also place your affirmations in this area or simply state them as you are enhancing it.

Be open and ready to experience renewed creativity in your life!

Once you have made changes to your Children and Creativity area or to an empty room, describe any shifts you notice in your life.

Chapter 5.8
Helpful People and Travel

HELPFUL PEOPLE
AND TRAVEL

Love brings gratitude,
inspiration for experiencing
wonderful places,
adventures, and
opportunities to meet
helpful people.

Like the Children and Creativity area, the Helpful People and Travel area spans many important facets of your life including travel, synchronicity, and support. If in Chapters 2 and 3 you identified your area of greatest need to be the freedom and ability to travel or to have an accessible and active support system, read on.

Feng Shui at Work

I recently did a consultation at a large financial office. My client had just moved to the area and was anxious to build his team. Outside his office were a number of empty cubicles awaiting his new staff, and his office was a vacant canvas. Such fun! We entered his office through the Helpful People and Travel area, so we worked with the wall behind the door. Upon my recommendation, he installed a metal file organizer in this area and filled it with gray file folders for each of the eight specific roles/team members he needed to hire. He filled them with information about the organization and added files to hold the business cards of mentors and recruiting agencies. He has been on a hiring spree since the consultation and has over half of his team in place. He is on his way!

Let Helpful People and Travel Be the Key to Support and Synchronicity

In the Feng Shui Bagua, the Helpful People and Travel area is in the front right corner of your home or business.

WEALTH PROSPERITY	FAME REPUTATION	LOVE MARRIAGE RELATIONSHIPS
HEALTH FAMILY FRIENDS	CENTER GROUNDING	CHILDREN CREATIVITY
KNOWLEDGE SELF-CULTIVATION	CAREER	HELPFUL PEOPLE AND TRAVEL

↑　　　　　↑　　　　　↑

ENTRANCE QUADRANT

In the *I Ching*, the Helpful People and Travel area is called "heaven." When everything is aligned, people and places give us the inspiration and guidance we need. This is total synchronicity . . . everything falling into the best place possible!

The Elements for Helpful People and Travel

The elements for the Helpful People and Travel area are Metal and Earth. Representations of the Metal element such as rocks and natural crystals work well here, as do circular shapes and white, gray, and pastel colors. Adding representations of the Earth element such as ceramics, rectangular shapes, and earth tones works with the Metal element to enhance creativity.

Interior Enhancements for the Helpful People and Travel Area of Your Home or Business (Choose One or More)

- Items in the colors white, black, or gray and circular in shape
- Art, photos, or figures pertaining to spiritual guides, mentors, or helpful people
- Photos or mementos of special places where you have traveled or want to travel
- Items made of metal such as furniture, lamps, frames, figurines
- Quotes, and affirmations pertaining to synchronicity, helpful people and travel

Exterior Enhancements for the Helpful People and Travel Area (Choose One or More)

- Items and flowers in the color white
- Garden art representing spiritual guides (angels, saints, Buddhas, etc.)
- Rocks and stones

What to Avoid in the Helpful People and Travel Area

- Too much of the color red, animal prints, and cone or triangle shapes representing the Fire element, which melts metal
- Anything that blocks synchronicity such as piles of clutter, unopened mail, dead or dying plants

A Helpful People and Travel Area Not Located Within the Bagua

If your Helpful People and Travel area is missing from your floor plan, you can anchor the area by applying one or a combination of the cures described in Chapter 6.

Feng Shui at Work

In a few salons I visit in town, I notice that their waiting area and metal product display shelves are in their Helpful People and Travel area. This is a very auspicious placement because their clients are their helpful people, and comfort and product placement are critical to their thriving businesses. This is called excellent intuitive Feng Shui!

A client recently bought a new home she planned to renovate. She was thrilled because it was almost rectangular with the Wealth and Prosperity and Love, Marriage, and Relationships areas intact. She did notice that it was missing the Helpful People and Travel area, but at the time did not think much about it, being swept away by location, price, and the cuteness factor. Soon after it closed escrow, all her renovation plans went awry. Contractors were not showing up, costs were higher than expected, appliances were breaking down. Problems also began occurring in her job, she had issues with her health insurance, and more. Her synchronicity was off. She reached out to me for help. I had her anchor her Helpful People and Travel area both inside and outside her home. Outside she anchored the area with a large plant with white blooms in a round white pot and replaced a small dead tree with a beautiful flowering tree that she encircled with flowering plants. Inside she hung a round mirror and a round faceted glass crystal on the wall closest to the missing area to help anchor the corner by symbolically closing it off. She also hung a picture of a gray and white mountain to represent the Metal element and added affirmations visualizing a successfully completed project. Within a month, she was able to finish the renovations and move in. Soon after, she was offered a lucrative new job. She now loves her home and her job.

It's time to enhance your Helpful People and Travel area to access its energy for solutions to your problems or the fulfillment of your travel dreams.

A Garage in the Helpful People and Travel Area

In most homes, such as ours, the garage is in the front right corner, the Helpful People and Travel area of the Bagua. Because this area is extremely powerful in making things happen in your life, it is imperative to keep your garage neat and clutter free if it is located in this corner. In our garage, we hung a large round faceted crystal in the center and brought in travel photos and images of our spiritual guides. We also created a vision board inside one of the cupboard doors with pictures and positive affirmations of what we want to have come into our lives.

Outside, in a small flower garden by the garage, we planted white flowers around a small white statue of an angel with his hands up to his mouth, blowing kisses toward our house. I like the symbolism of him sending positive energy our way. Whenever we feel that our synchronicity is off and we keep hitting stumbling blocks, I say, "Honey, it's time to clean the garage." We take a few hours to organize, dust, polish, sweep, and restate our affirmations. We immediately feel the shift in energy, and our garage becomes pleasing to look at again.

Longing to Travel

Where are you going this year? Do you have the travel bug? Are you dreaming of exotic faraway places, fun family vacations, or even peaceful retreats? How do you get there? How do you make it happen?

I love looking back on a memorable trip to Stockholm and Paris that my husband and I took years ago, enjoying a cruise of the Stockholm archipelago, viewing the Paris lights from a boat on the Seine, people watching while sipping wine in cafés. I think about this joyous time and reflect on what made this magical trip possible. I believe that positive affirmations and enhancements in the Helpful People and Travel area of our home played a large role.

Even when I teach Feng Shui classes, I use the Bagua to enhance the classroom to support my travel dreams. Students in my classes notice that I have pictures of France everywhere: the Eiffel Tower in the Helpful People and Travel area;

the dark Seine River at night in Career; a Paris flower mart and vineyards in Knowledge and Self-Cultivation and in Health, Family, and Friends; lavender fields in Wealth and Prosperity; and red poppy fields in Fame and Reputation. Every Bagua area is represented by my favorite parts of France.

Whether you desire to go on an exotic holiday, a local vacation, or want to ensure that everything goes smoothly during an upcoming move or on your everyday commute to work, Feng Shui can help. Feng Shui is simply about living in harmony with the world around you. When your environment is harmonious, channels are open for good things to come your way.

Feng Shui as a Travel Companion

When planning to travel, two especially important things to consider are visualizing your trip and activating Feng Shui energy while you are traveling.

Visualizing Your Trip

To help you achieve your travel goals, the first thing you want to do is declutter, activate, and enhance the Helpful People and Travel area of your home. As in every other facet of life, you achieve your goals when you focus clearly on what you want. Therefore, visualize it and it will happen. Positive affirmations, enhancements, imagery, and vision boards in the Helpful People and Travel area can be very effective in helping you get to where you want to go. (See suggestions below for how to build an ideal travel vision board.) Collecting pictures or travel brochures of your dream destination, visualizing yourself relaxing on a beautiful soft sandy beach in Hawaii, climbing Half Dome in Yosemite, or just having a stress-free daily commute to work will begin the energy flow.

Feng Shui at Work

A client has become a master at creating vision boards for herself. She has many affirmations and pictures on them related to her jewelry business. She hired a new rep, and her beautiful pieces are featured in numerous stores. Business is booming, and she even had an opportunity to travel to Milan, Italy, to show her jewelry at Fashion Week.

Another client had "traveling to Egypt to see the pyramids" on her bucket list. After a consultation, she created a vision board with pictures of the pyramids, travel brochures, and inspirational sayings to keep in her Helpful People and Travel area. She took it a step further and placed either a mini replica of a pyramid or a small picture of one in the front right corner of every room in her house. With her affirmations and visualization, she made it happen! She just returned from her once-in-a-lifetime, fabulous trip to Egypt.

Create a Travel Vision Board. Creating a vision board or dream board is an excellent way to give imagery to your goals. To start, make a collage of pictures, words, and phrases that reflect where you want to travel and how you want to feel when you get there. Put pictures of yourself in the scenario. Act as if you're already there.

Because the Helpful People and Travel area is enhanced by the Metal element, you can use white poster board with a black border or in a black metal frame, add black-and-white photos, foreign coins, and/or a small metal figure like the Eiffel Tower. Finally, write your affirmations on the board and repeat them on a regular basis as if they have already happened. For best Feng Shui, trust your feelings. Experiment and play around with your board until you reach that moment when everything clicks, and you have the perfect vision board to support your dreams. Keep it in the Helpful People and Travel area of your home and look at it every day.

Activating Feng Shui Energy While Traveling

The key to good travel Feng Shui is to bring it with you internally as well as externally by packing a few enhancing items for spaces you will temporarily be occupying. Because Feng Shui is about creating harmony with the world around you, there's no better time to step up your travel Feng Shui than while you are in transit, either at or between destinations.

In her book *The Western Guide to Feng Shui*, Terah Kathryn Collins goes into detail on how to create a Feng Shui Travel Kit[2]. My daughter liked this idea so much that she created a kit she gave to me as a gift. The following are excerpts from the book, with some of my personal examples.

Create a Feng Shui Travel Kit. Following Terah's advice, on trips I always bring a soft Feng Shui travel pouch filled with the following items:

- A small diagram of the Bagua
- One or more round faceted crystals on strings
- Four small items in white, red, purple, and green or blue to place in each of the corresponding corners of the room: white in Helpful People and Travel; purple in Wealth and Prosperity; red in Love, Marriage, and Relationships; and green or blue in Knowledge and Self-Cultivation
- Four tea lights (scented ones are nice) in their own metal or plastic cups
- Cleansing incense, such as pine or sandalwood
- Thumbtacks, safety pins, matches, string
- A multicolored scarf with colors that represent the Five Elements (white, black, green or blue, yellow, and red hues)
- A smooth stone or natural crystal for grounding energy
- A touchstone that reminds me physically and emotionally of home, such as a picture of loved ones or another item from home

Start at the front door of your hotel room or rental house or apartment. Referring to the Bagua, place one crystal in front of a window; place blues, greens, or

---

2   *The Western Guide to Feng Shui* ©1996. All Rights Reserved.

florals in the Health, Family, and Friends area; purple tones in Wealth and Prosperity; white in Helpful People and Travel; and red, white, and/or pink in the Love, Marriage, and Relationships area. If the room feels especially stagnant, hang a crystal in the center of the room. Set up a place of beauty in the area you see when you wake up. You can really energize this space by laying a cloth or scarf that contains the colors of all the Five Elements and adding incense, candles, and fresh flowers when available.

Move the furniture if necessary. You can also use a towel or your Five-Element scarf to cover the TV, which is usually a big hunk of energy staring down at the bed. As always, make sure to keep the room clutter free.

Figure 31 Feng Shui Travel Kit

Creating a personalized space for ourselves in temporary environments allows us to center, unwind, and fully enjoy the fun of traveling stress free.

Feng Shui at Work

While on our last trip to Paris, my husband and I rented a lovely one-bedroom apartment. It had four big windows with large window boxes along the right side. The apartment was artfully decorated and charming, but the window boxes contained dead flowers, all working to drain our energy. I took it upon myself to go on a fun shopping trip to a local flower market where I bought a flat of red petunias to plant in each box. For the remainder of our stay, the Ch'i was enhanced and worked to make the trip highly successful, fun, and hassle free.

Sample Affirmations for the Helpful People and Travel Area

- "I am surrounded by helpful people. Whenever I have a problem, they're there."
- "I love to travel and am blessed with many opportunities."
- "My commute is a breeze. I find ways to make the most of my travel time and I return home energized and happy."

Feng Shui on a Shoestring

Placing a written affirmation with a picture of your intended travel location in the front right corner of your home or in every room is a very inexpensive way to make your travel dreams come true. Another cost-effective way to energize your travel goals is to create a vision board.

The wonderful thing about creating a vision board is that you can put it together with anything you have around your home: snapshots, drawings, magazine photos or photos downloaded from the computer, and any kind of background poster board, paper, and cloth imaginable. See Chapter 7 for more information on how to create a vision board.

Feng Shui can be the solution to your travel dreams and some of your problems. The Helpful People and Travel corner is the best place to start.

Your Turn

What is working, and what feels misaligned in your life? What would change in your life if you had more "helpful people" or a stronger support network?

Where would you like to travel? What would it feel like to travel there? What would traveling mean to you?

Find your Helpful People and Travel area on the Bagua. What room is located there? How is it decorated? Describe it in detail: colors, elements, decorations, art. Is it in good condition? If it is outside the structure, what is there now?

Does this area contain items that are broken, messy, or out of place? Clear the area of these items first for a quick win.

Make a note of the items in this area that are nurturing your attraction of helpful people and your ability to travel. Make another note of the items that are hindering them.

What can you do with the items that are hindering your attraction of helpful people and your ability to travel? Clean or repair them? Give them away? Move them to a more appropriate room?

List the enhancements you want to make to this area. Check them off as you complete them!

Bless your new space and write your affirmations below. You can also place your affirmations in the area or simply state them as you are enhancing it.

Be open and ready to experience more synchronicity and fun travel experiences!

Once you have made changes in this area, describe any shifts you notice in your life.

Chapter 5.9
Center and Grounding

CENTER AND
GROUNDING

With love I feel grounded
and aligned with
the Universe.
Life flows and centers all!

Now it is time to address the hub of the wheel, the core of the Bagua. This is not one of the eight trigrams but is the Center of them. This area is meant to ground and energize the other areas of your life. If your area of greatest need is to live a balanced life that is grounded, centered, focused, and in harmony with your life goals, this is where you want to begin.

Feng Shui at Work

When your life feels as if there is a lack of structure, that you cannot move forward and are unable to shake an overwhelming floaty, wishy-washy feeling, you may be experiencing a lack of the grounding Earth element in your environment. This recently happened to a client of mine who was trying to feel grounded, organized, and stable while her environment was working against her. She was living on a boat, which, though beautiful, was naturally surrounded by water. This made staying grounded even more trying since much of the boat was white and metal, representing the Metal element, which holds Water. She was experiencing the chaos of floating, unable to get back to both her artwork and the community she loved. In Feng Shui, the Five Elements (Water, Wood, Fire, Earth, and Metal) work to balance each other (see Chapter 8). What she needed to do was incorporate into her environment strong representations of the Earth element, which helps to dam and control Water. To accomplish this, we added rectangular paintings of her own along with other art representing her community; rectangular pillows with maps of the city she wished to return to; and lots of earth tones and ceramics. Within a week she serendipitously found the perfect living situation in the community she loves, for less than she was paying for the boat. It even has a studio for her to continue the art she excels at. She now feels more grounded and has come out of her uncertain chaos. She so loved how Feng Shui helped her that she used its principles to enhance her new rental. Success continued to follow her—she sold the boat and recently bought the perfect home which she remodeled to fit her needs. Feng Shui worked for her!

The more I delve into the world of Feng Shui, the more grounded I feel. I have had the pleasure of helping many clients enhance their homes, have met many enthusiastic learners in my classes, and have enjoyed sharing this knowledge with readers of my columns. Together we have learned to balance the elements and the importance of the eight trigrams of the Bagua in our lives, plus the ever-important Center.

In the Feng Shui Bagua, the Center area is, well, in the center of your home or business.

WEALTH PROSPERITY	FAME REPUTATION	LOVE MARRIAGE RELATIONSHIPS
HEALTH FAMILY FRIENDS	CENTER GROUNDING	CHILDREN CREATIVITY
KNOWLEDGE SELF-CULTIVATION	CAREER	HELPFUL PEOPLE AND TRAVEL

↑   ↑   ↑

ENTRANCE QUADRANT

In the *I Ching*, the Center area of your home or business is meant to be the core where all other areas connect. It is a peaceful area, to help you stay centered and grounded.

The Element for the Center

The element for the Center is Earth, which is represented by the soil. The Earth element suggests the importance of stabilizing your life. It is represented by adobe, brick, tile, ceramic, or earthenware objects; the shapes are rectangles and squares; art and colors in yellow and brown rust tones.

Interior Enhancements for the Center Area of Your Home or Business (Choose One or More)

- Items in yellow and earth tones and in square or rectangular shapes
- Art or photos representing landscapes, people, or subjects in the color yellow
- A gallery wall of family pictures in rectangular frames
- Ceramics or pottery
- Quotes, affirmations, and sayings pertaining to feeling grounded and centered

Exterior Enhancements for the Center Area of Your Home or Business (Choose One or More)

- A courtyard, patio, or atrium
- Items, flowers, plants in the yellow spectrum
- Ceramic garden art such as tiles, statuary, fountains, pots, and benches
- Square or rectangular shapes

What to Avoid in the Center Area

- Too much of the Water element, which creates a muddied effect when combined with the Earth element

Sample Affirmations for the Center Area

- "I feel centered and grounded at all times."
- "I am at peace with myself and my decisions."

- "I am safe and comfortable on the earth."
- "My body moves with balance and ease."

Feng Shui at Work

Many people have the kitchen in the center of their home. This is an extremely auspicious location because the kitchen is known as the "hearth" of a home and can feed the soul and act as a grounding force. My daughter had her kitchen in this location and painted it a saffron color, enhancing it with ceramic tiles, yellow candles, and art in the gold spectrum. The feeling was so cheery it became the heart of her home.

A Stairwell in the Center Area

Oftentimes a stairwell or bathroom will occupy the Center space. Although neither are optimum, enhancements can be made to offset negative energy. Stairwells tend to draw the Ch'i down or pull the Ch'i out. Therefore, mirrors or a round faceted crystal can be placed at the bottom of the stairs to send the flow of energy back up to circulate throughout the home. The walls can be enhanced with earth-tone pictures hung horizontally, not stair-stepped down.

Feng Shui at Work

Stairs in the center of a home can have the effect of drawing energy downward. We have this situation in our home. To enhance the area, we painted it a soft yellow, decorated the landing with earth-tone vases, and hung earth-tone art along the stairwell in a horizontal line. (Art that is hung in a descending or stair-stepped fashion increases the energy draw downward.) We also hung a mirror at the bottom of the stairs to slow the flow of energy. This beautifully enhanced stairwell at the back of our entrance foyer has become one of my favorite areas in the home. It helps to center me every time I enter it.

Figure 32 Hallway stairs in Center-walls painted a soft yellow

Figure 33 Small mirror hung at the bottom of the staircase

A Bathroom in the Center Area

Remember that in bathrooms, the toilets should be kept closed when not in use. A 30 millimeter round faceted crystal hung in the center of the bathroom also helps to circulate the Ch'i. A bathroom in the Center area benefits from ceramics, art, wall colors in the yellow spectrum, and rectangular and square shapes.

Feng Shui on a Shoestring

Placing a ceramic vase or rectangular ceramic trivet in the center area of your home, especially in earth-tone shades, will calm the space and help you to feel more grounded.

Surround yourself with the centering qualities of the Earth element and enjoy the support you need for a happy life.

Feng Shui at Work

A client recently asked me to help create a landscape for their backyard. They felt that their yard with a gorgeous view was not inviting to their guests. The house happened to be U-shaped, and the missing area was in the Center and Fame and Reputation areas of their property. I recommended using beautiful ceramic pavers for the patio and building a small brick retaining wall. They wanted to create a welcoming area in the center of the patio by adding a fire pit. To further enhance the Fame and Reputation area and feed the Earth element with Fire, I recommended adding comfortable chairs with red-tone cushions and placing yellow and red plants in ceramic pots all around. Their backyard has become a showcase and a "hub" for entertaining guests.

Your Turn

Do you feel centered, grounded, and balanced in your life? What is missing? What would feeling centered, grounded, and balanced look and feel like to you?

Find your Center area on the Bagua. What room is located there? How is it decorated? Describe it in detail: colors, elements, decorations, art. Is it in good condition? If it is outside the structure, what is there now?

Does this area contain items that are broken, messy, or out of place? Clear the area of these items first for a quick win.

Make a note of the items in this area that are nurturing your ability to feel centered, grounded, and balanced. Make another note of the items that are hindering it.

What can you do with the items that are hindering your ability to feel centered, grounded, and balanced? Clean and repair them? Give them away? Move them to a more appropriate room?

List the enhancements you want to make to this area. Check them off as you complete them!

Bless your new space and write your affirmations below. You can also place your affirmations in the area or simply state them as you are enhancing it.

Be open and ready to experience feeling centered, grounded, and balanced in your life!

Once you have made changes in this area, describe any shifts you notice in your life.

Chapter 6:
Step 6 - Anchor Missing Bagua Areas Outside and Inside the Structure

Feng Shui at Work

A client was remodeling a townhome located on an angular lot. She was very frustrated about the lack of synchronicity in her project. Materials were backordered, contractors were not showing up, estimates were coming in over budget. A quick mapping of her property showed that her Helpful People and Travel area was totally missing from the diagonal lot and was also not in her house's footprint. We located the missing corner of the house's Helpful People and Travel area in her front lawn, and since it wasn't in a space where she could plant a tree or place a boulder, she instead buried a large quartz crystal pointing upward, with a positive affirmation. She also placed affirmations and natural crystals in the front right corner of every room in her house. The project took on a different energy and was completed soon after to her pleasure and satisfaction.

The ideal shape for a house in Feng Shui is a square or rectangle. This means that all Bagua areas of the home are contained within the structure, and that the Ch'i can circulate through all the important areas of your life. Yet, more than 90 percent of Western homes are not perfectly rectangular. They may have areas outside the Bagua, which in Feng Shui are considered missing areas. When areas in your home are "missing" from the Bagua map, they could also be missing from your life.

Identify and Anchor Missing Corners

To begin, locate the four corners of your home. Are any corners missing from the rectangle of the Bagua map? If so, stand at the exact location where the two walls would have met and use the enhancements described below to either structurally or symbolically fill in or "anchor" the missing corner.

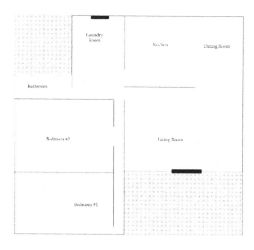

Figure 34 Home layout with two shaded missing areas

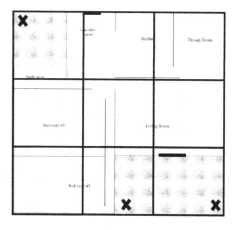

Figure 35 Bagua applied to layout-X's mark anchoring points

Anchoring Missing Corners of the Bagua Outside the Structure

Structurally. You can literally complete the missing area by adding a structure such as a room, porch, deck, arbor, trellis, and so on. The structure needs to have enough substance to be considered part of the building.

Figure 36 Structural anchoring by building a trellis across missing Bagua area

Figure 37 Lower view of trellis as anchor

<u>Symbolically</u>. You can also complete the missing area with a symbolic addition that defines the missing area with a large item such as (but not limited to):

- In Wealth and Prosperity: Anchor with a purple fountain, purple gazing ball, or a purple-leafed tree.

Figure 38 Purple fountain anchoring missing Wealth and Prosperity area

Figure 39 Purple gazing ball and flowers anchoring missing Wealth and Prosperity area

- In Love, Marriage, and Relationships: Anchor with a two-seat bistro set, large red flowering plant, red gazing ball, pairs of garden art representing romance.

Figure 40 Red gazing ball and flowers anchoring missing Love, Marriage, and Relationships area

Figure 41 Red and white bistro set anchoring missing Love, Marriage, and Relationships area

- In Helpful People and Travel: Anchor with a boulder, stone or metal sculpture of a spiritual guide, white metal seating, silver, or gold gazing ball, large white or gray round pots with white flowers, lighting.

Figure 42 White metal bench anchoring missing Helpful People and Travel area

Figure 43 Gold gazing ball anchoring missing Helpful People and Travel area

- In Knowledge and Self-Cultivation: Anchor with a large tree, statue, blue or green gazing ball, wooden seating, lighting.

Figure 44 Blue gazing ball anchoring the missing Knowledge and Self-Cultivation area

Feng Shui at Work

> **A client had a cute cottage with an open cement front porch in the Helpful People and Travel area. She anchored the edge of the patio with a large plant in a white, round pot. (Round shapes and the color white are both representations of the Metal element.) My client was able to rent the property for a great price and buy a larger home for her family.**

When Outside Room is Tight. If there is no room for a structural or large symbolic addition outside, anchor with one of the following in the missing corner:

- On the lawn. Bury a quartz crystal pointed upward in the specified corner.
- On cement. Mark the exact corner with a small symbol such as a heart for the Love, Marriage, and Relationships area; a tree for the Knowledge and Self-Cultivation area; a circle for the Helpful People and Travel area; or a triangle for the Wealth and Prosperity area

Anchoring Missing Corners of the Bagua Inside the Structure

Hanging a mirror on the wall closest to the missing Bagua area will help symbolically push the wall out to close off the missing corner. This can also be done by hanging a thirty millimeter, round faceted crystal in front of a window in the same wall. Use art and personal enhancements representing the Bagua area in this indented area to further enhance the Ch'i, especially pieces with depth.

Figure 45 Mirrors and photo of lavender flowers on wall
adjacent to missing Wealth and Prosperity area

Figure 46 Love representations in the back right corner of another room in the house

Anchoring Missing Middle Top, Bottom, and Side Areas Outside the Structure

Sometimes houses have missing Bagua areas in the middle, front, back, or sides of the structure, as well as missing corners. The goal is to anchor or complete every missing area with something significant that is in harmony with your home. Choose items and designs that represent the elements of the Bagua area you are anchoring, giving them the dual purpose of anchoring the missing area, as well as enhancing it.

Here are a few suggestions.

- In Career: Anchor with water features such as fountains, waterfalls, vibrant plants, black shiny pots.
- In Health, Family, and Friends: Anchor with wooden seating and a colorful flower garden.
- In Fame and Reputation: Anchor with red plants and bright lighting, a barbecue grill, fire pit, red chairs, or cushions.
- In Children and Creativity: Anchor with metal seating, sculptures, whimsical garden art, large rocks, or gravel paths.
- In the Center (which might be missing in a U-shaped home where the entrance is deep in the center): Anchor with ceramic tiles, brickwork, rectangular shapes, ceramic pots, earth-tone garden art, and flowers.

Anchoring Missing Middle Top, Bottom, and Side Areas Inside the Structure

As with anchoring these areas outside the structure, choose significant items that are in harmony with your home and that represent the elements of the Bagua area you are anchoring. Begin by anchoring these missing areas inside your home by hanging a mirror or thirty millimeter, round faceted glass crystal on the wall adjacent to the missing area. Both of these enhancements act as cures to symbolically close off the missing area. If there is room, add a piece of art on the wall that reflects the Bagua area. Some ideas for art anchors:

- In Career: Anchor with art depicting moving water.
- In Health, Family, and Friends: Anchor with art depicting vibrant flowers.
- In Fame and Reputation: Anchor with art in shades of red, representing upward movement, celebration, sun, stars.
- In Children and Creativity: Anchor with whimsical art or art depicting children in pastel shades.
- In the Center: Anchor with art in earth tones, such as sunflowers, wheat fields, yellow trees.

Enhance the Missing Bagua Area in Every Room

When a Bagua area is missing from the house structure, it is important to locate and enhance that same area in every room. For instance, if the Love, Marriage, and Relationships area is missing in your house and you want to increase romance, place the Bagua at the entrance of each room; locate the Love, Marriage, and Relationships area in the back right corner; and place something red, or a pair of items, or a picture of a couple or other representation of romance there.

Sample Affirmations for Anchoring a Missing Bagua Area

- "The energy is staying within my home; prosperity is flowing my way."
- "I have captured the energy flowing into my love life, and am in a committed, loving relationship."
- "The energy is staying within my Helpful People and Travel area, and I feel the support of others."
- "Closing the missing Knowledge and Self-Cultivation corner has brought me more peace."
- "My career is flourishing. I love my job."
- "I am strong and healthy."
- "My reputation has never been better."
- "I feel energized and creative. My children are thriving."
- "This house grounds me."

Feng Shui on a Shoestring

The art of anchoring can mean simply moving a mirror, a piece of art, a seating arrangement, sculpture, or large rock from one area of your home to the missing area. And enhancing the process with affirmations is always free!

Your home should nurture all aspects of your life. Keeping the Ch'i vibrant and flowing within your home keeps you surrounded and nourished with the positive energy you need to thrive. Once you have anchored and enhanced areas missing from the Bagua map, enjoy the benefits of a positive energy flow, and express gratitude for all your blessings.

Your Turn

What areas of your home are missing from the Bagua and need anchoring?

What is in those areas now?

How are these missing areas affecting your life?

Can these areas be anchored structurally by building a trellis, deck, room addition, and so on?

Can they be anchored symbolically by adding a seating arrangement, gazing ball, boulder, tree, large plant, sculpture, etc.?

What can you do to anchor these areas from inside the house?

List the anchoring steps you want to take in these areas. Check them off as you complete them!

Bless your new space and write your affirmations below. You can also place your affirmations in the area or simply state them as you are anchoring it.

Be open and ready to experience renewed energy and opportunities in those areas of your life now anchored in your Bagua.

Once you have anchored these areas, describe any shifts you notice in your life.

Chapter 7:
Step 7 - Create a Vision Board

A very important Feng Shui tool for achieving one's goals is visualization. Feng Shui believes that when you picture what you want to have happen, the more likely it is to happen. Feng Shui is a blend of physical "seen" enhancements and mental "unseen" intentions. When you intend to bring about changes in your life by making enhancements to your home, the powers of affirmation and visualization will help those enhancements manifest your intention.

An easy and fun way to visualize the achievement of your goals is to create a vision board. Vision boards are a collection of images, words, and objects that represent your hopes and dreams. They depict images of where you want to be and what you want to happen. Here are the steps for creating a vision board:

- Begin with a board (11x14 or 8 ½x14 are the most practical sizes, but anything goes).
- Think of your life in the course of a year, a season or an event, or an even loftier lifetime goal. Then close your eyes and visualize exactly what you want to happen and how you want to feel.
- Cut out images from magazines, calendars, maps, postcards, and photos that represent these goals.
- You can make your board three-dimensional by adding glitter, string, stickers, shells, rocks, magnets, beads, and so on. Remember that you have freedom of expression in creating your board.
- Use a glue stick, glue gun, tacks, white glue, tape, etc. to affix items to the board.
- Add inspirational words that are very specific to your goals. Words are very powerful; they turn ideas into action. Therefore, keep them in the affirmative and use positive, uplifting statements only. Focus on what you want your life to look and feel like, not what is happening now. Picture

what achieving your goals would feel like and use words and pictures to capture that feeling.

- Add specific affirmations that you write yourself, as if the goal has already been achieved.
- If you want to create a board with quantitative goals, add a sticker dot to each one as you achieve it. (A real estate agent had a goal of selling ten homes one season. She placed a dot on her board each time she sold one. This way she could honor her achievements and watch her goal manifest itself.)
- **Note:** Vision board software also exists if you are more digitally savvy and do not want to cut and paste. You can create a slideshow vision board on PowerPoint and have it running in a digital frame that you can look at all day. To learn more, go to

https://www.developgoodhabits.com/online-vision-board/

You also can create a vision board for a single long-term goal as a continual reminder to stay on track. For example, if your ultimate goal is to become president of a company, when making decisions in your daily life, ask yourself, "Is this what the president of a company would do?"

These are but guidelines; there is no right or wrong in creating a vision board. It is a personal representation of your goals. Therefore, it has to speak to you. It is intended to be big and bold and to break you out of your perceived limitations.

Feng Shui at Work

In 2008, my daughter created a vision board with the goals of working at Toyota and owning real estate. Both came true by 2012! Since
that time, she has created more vision boards for career advancement
goals, and all have been achieved.

Clients of mine have a very important business, empowering wom-
en to love themselves and to overcome disruptive love patterns when
choosing their soul mate. One very powerful tool they teach their clients to use is a Love vision board. I have had the pleasure of doing
Feng Shui consultations for many of their clients, and each time I see
beautiful, personalized vision boards depicting love, empowerment,
soul mates, and marriage. Many of these clients have found their soul
mates and have gotten married. There is so much power in visualizing
your dreams using vision boards. www.johnnyandlara.com

Connecting Your Vision Board to the Bagua

The Feng Shui Bagua map helps you locate specific energies in your home.
Using the Bagua map as a template for your vision board helps you connect
your goals to the specific areas of need located in your home.

No matter what your goal is, placing a picture, an affirmation, or an inspiring
word on your vision board in the corresponding area of the Bagua map will
make their energy more powerful.

WEALTH PROSPERITY	FAME REPUTATION	LOVE MARRIAGE RELATIONSHIPS
HEALTH FAMILY FRIENDS	CENTER GROUNDING	CHILDREN CREATIVITY
KNOWLEDGE SELF-CULTIVATION	CAREER	HELPFUL PEOPLE AND TRAVEL

↑　　　　↑　　　　↑

ENTRANCE QUADRANT

Sample Vision Board Enhancements for Each Bagua Area

- Career: The power to achieve your career goals (black or very dark colors, images of glass/crystal items, water features)
- Knowledge and Self-Cultivation: Personal growth, honoring the ability to self- enrich and be at peace (images of items made of wood, blue and green colors, pictures of tranquil wooded landscapes and trees)
- Health, Family, and Friends: Strength, vitality, growth (images of items made of wood; blue and green colors; pictures of trees, flowering plants, people in a healthy state)
- Wealth and Prosperity: Gratitude and abundance (images of opulent items in the purple color spectrum, healthy and round-leaved plants)

- Fame and Reputation: Integrity, how you are seen, where you glow (red, items representing the Fire element with candles and lighting, personal awards)
- Love, Marriage, and Relationships: Receptivity and intimacy (images of items in pairs, art or photos depicting romance, reds and pink colors)
- Children and Creativity: What makes you happy, childlike, creative (images of metal items, white and pastel colors, whimsical art, pictures of children)
- Helpful People and Travel: Synchronicity, being at the right place at the right time (art or images of spiritual guides, angels, mentors; images of metal items; white, black, or gray colors)
- Center: Grounding and centering (images of ceramics, yellow and earth-tone colors, rectangle shapes)

Keep the vital energy in your board by pointing words and pictures toward the Center, which represents you. If you want a boost of energy focused on one area of your board—in Love, Marriage, and Relationships, for example—point your words and pictures toward that area.

You're done! Display your board in a location where you will see it every day. This will keep you grounded, keep you focused, help you grow, and remind you of what you are grateful for. It will help you create order out of chaos. Once you have achieved the goals envisioned on your board, update it or create a new board for a new year or a new project. Enjoy the journey of the unfolding of your life.

I always create a vision board whenever we start a home construction project. For instance, when we began a renovation project in our kitchen, I created a board with these enhancements:

- In the Center, I placed a colored version of our architectural plan on a yellow background, representing the finished product and grounding element. I placed pictures and affirmations in all areas of the Bagua, all pointing to the Center.

- In Knowledge and Self-Cultivation, most important for this project, I placed the business card of our contractor.
- In Health, Family, and Friends, I placed pictures of our new wooden cabinets.
- In Wealth and Prosperity, I placed a log of our budget and the word affordable.
- In Fame and Reputation, I placed pictures of our lighting.
- In Love, Marriage, and Relationships, I placed pictures of a pair of items, as well as the words "We Love our Kitchen."
- In Children and Creativity, I placed the card of our designer.
- In Helpful People and Travel, I placed the names of all the friends and contractors who have advised us and worked on the project. Additional words such as "Completed, Easy Remodel, New and Improved" appear as well.
- In Career, I placed a picture of our black appliances.

The minute we hung the board, in a place where I could see it daily, we felt a shift in energy. We met with a plumbing supply company that gave us a great price for our sink and fixtures, the designer came up with a beautiful new style of oak door that we love, and we got an appointment with a tile company to view the four designs of granite we had shifted to. This company also had back-splash designers. Suddenly, things began to click. I'm happy to say that our project was very successful. I'm sold on vision boards!

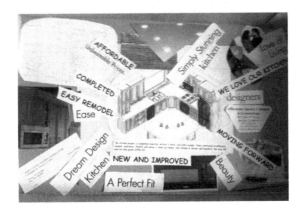

Figure 47 Vision board for a successful kitchen remodeling project

If I or any of my friends and family are experiencing health issues, going in for tests or surgery, I create a vision board to place in the Health, Family, and Friends area of our home next to a flowering plant or vase of fresh flowers. The board would contain pictures of healthy, thriving people and pictures of flowers and words such as "Healthy, Thriving, Healed." I would also add an affirmation stating what I want to have happen. "The tests came out negative." "The surgery was successful." "I am healthy and thriving." Placing a picture of the person in a happy, healthy state near the board further energizes the intent. Once the message on the board is achieved, I transition the plant to the garden and remove the board.

Figure 48 Vibrant flowers and vision board for good health

Sample Affirmations for Vision Boards

- "I have found my soul mate."
- "I am thriving in my dream job."
- "I awake with joy and purpose every day."
- "The remodeling project has been completed smoothly and within budget."
- Visualizing and affirming success will help make your dreams come true.

By now you have learned the steps necessary for enhancing the Bagua areas of your home using the Five Elements to optimize energy flow. Perhaps you are already feeling a shift and beginning to reap the benefits.

The next, and eighth step of your journey to empowerment through Feng Shui is to balance the Five Elements and Yin and Yang energy in your home.

Your Turn

What area of your life could benefit from a vision board? Picture what it would look like.

Find the Bagua area in your home where you would place your vision board. What room is located there?

Describe in detail what you would place on your vision board: colors, elements, decorations, art, sayings.

After you hang your vision board, what affirmations could you make to help activate the energy?

Bless your new space and write your affirmations below. You can also place your affirmations in the area or simply state them as you are enhancing it.

Be open and ready to experience movement toward achieving your goals.

Once you have created and displayed your vision board, describe any shifts you notice in your life.

Chapter 8:
Step 8 - Balance the Five Elements and Yin Yang Energy

Have You Heard This?

"Every time I enter your office, I want to stay there and take it all in. It feels peaceful, harmonious, and meetings held there are always productive and pleasant. The positive energy makes it a space where people enjoy gathering."

On the Other Hand, Have You Thought This?

"My bedroom is gray and monochromatic. It feels cold and uninviting. I don't want to stay there long. Come to think of it, my love life feels about the same; not many sparks or fire."

What makes these two environments so different? *Elemental Balance!*

Feng Shui at Work

While on vacation, I had the opportunity to do a consultation at a friend's house who happened to live in a beautiful log cabin. She asked me to help her balance all the wood in her environment that was making her feel stuck. I told her that what her home needed was some representation of the Metal element—the controlling element of Wood. I suggested a cream couch, with rounded arms and back, pastel linens and a cream-colored carpet, as whites and pastels are representations of the Metal element. We added bronze lamps and natural rocks. To strengthen the Metal element even more, we brought in some Earth which nourishes Metal, in the form of a large yellow candle on the coffee table. We avoided adding any dark colors or water features because we did not want to feed the Wood with Water. These simple additions produced great results! Her home looks amazing and has a truly revitalizing feel to it. Consequently, she has had a renewed burst of energy.

Balancing the Five Elements in Your Home or Business

Thousands of years ago, the early Feng Shui practitioners discovered that harmony existed where the elements of Water, Wood, Fire, Earth, and Metal were all present.

The office described on page 207 feels peaceful and productive because it is elementally balanced, while the bedroom feels cold and uninviting because it is elementally imbalanced, dominated by representations of metal. We are most comfortable when all five elements are harmoniously represented in a home or workplace.

To achieve perfect harmony in your home, each of the Bagua areas needs to be elementally balanced. Here is a step-by-step guide to achieving that balance:

- Identify the elements in a room.
- Note the quantity of each and assess the need for adjustments.
- Add or subtract elements as necessary to establish balance.

Identifying the Elements

The use of elements does not have to be literal. As previously discussed, elements can be represented in colors, shapes, art, and textiles. Below is a list of representations for each of the Five Elements.

Water

- Colors: Black or very dark colors
- Shapes: Asymmetrical
- Items: Water features such as fountains or aquariums; glass, crystal, mirrors
- Art: Water scenes such as oceans, lakes, and ponds

Wood

- Colors: Blue, green
- Shapes: Columns or vertical stripes
- Items: Wooden items, plants (real or artificial), plant-based cloth, books, paper items, images of fruits and vegetables
- Art: Wooded scenes such as forests, meadows, gardens; floral art

Fire

- Colors: Red spectrum including pinks, reddish orange, and purple
- Shapes: Cones, pyramids, triangles, flame shapes
- Items: All lighting, including natural light and candles; fireplaces, barbecue grills; items derived from animals such as fur, leather, feathers, bone
- Art: Depicting people, animals, fire, suns, stars; printed words; numbers

Earth

- Colors: Yellows, browns, earth tones
- Shapes: Square and rectangular
- Items: Ceramics, adobe, bricks, earthenware items
- Art: Earth-tone pictures such as yellow landscapes, deserts, sunflowers

Metal

- Colors: White, gray, pastels
- Shapes: Circles, globes, curved arches
- Items: All items made of metal, natural stone, natural crystals
- Art: Representing mountains, stones, or anything in the shades of gray and white

Many items may contain more than one element. For instance, a yellow and red flower would represent three elements: Wood–the plant; Earth–the yellow color; Fire–the red color. It is important to take your time to really look at each item to recognize all the represented elements. Working with the elements can be fun and rewarding. Knowing how they affect your life is key to learning how to arrange them.

How the Five Elements Affect Your life

At the Western School of Feng Shui™, Terah Kathryn Collins teaches the influence the Five Elements have on your life.[3]

<u>Water</u>   *Represented by a body of water*

- In balance: Enhances communication, inspiration, calm, ease
- Too much: Lack of structure, wishy-washy
- Too little: Competition, stress, lack of communication and connections

<u>Wood</u>   *Represented by the tree*

- In balance: Enhances trust, originality, spirituality, new growth, ideas
- Too much: Overwhelmed feeling of overexpansion, stretched too thin
- Too little: Sluggishness, lack of creativity

<u>Fire</u>   *Represented by the hearth*

- In balance: Enhances excitement, enthusiasm, leadership, personal warmth
- Too much: Amplifies aggression and impatience
- Too little: Lack of positive movement, cold

<u>Metal</u>   *Represented by the minerals in the earth*

- In balance: Enhances mental clarity, presence of mind, prioritizing skills
- Too much: Causes rigidity, closed-mindedness
- Too little: Creates indecisiveness, procrastination

---

3   From course materials, Western School of Feng Shui™. All Rights Reserved.

<u>Earth</u>   *Represented by the soil*

- In balance: Enhances a feeling of being grounded, balanced, organized, stable
- Too much: Overly disciplined and conservative
- Too little: Feelings of spaciness and chaos

Assessing Your Needs

Once you have made enhancements to your areas of need based on the Bagua map, step back and assess the elements that are at play in each area. I like to use a table such as the one on the following pages to list the elements in a room and what they represent. Recognize that items can represent combinations of elements. For instance, a wooden chair (wood) when painted red represents both fire and wood, but if painted black represents water and wood. Once you have completed your list, pay attention to what is dominant and what there is too little of in each Bagua area.

Feng Shui Element Assessment Guide

One easy way to assess Feng Shui elemental balance is to stand in a room and make a quick list of all the elements you see. Many items may contain more than one element. Once you've completed your list, you will be able to assess whether one element dominates, or if some are missing or are underrepresented.

Pick a room and use the tables in the following pages[4] to list all of the items you have that represent each element. Make copies of them so you can use them in more than one room or write assessments for each room on separate pieces of paper. For example, a rectangular gray couch would be listed under these elements:

- Metal: Gray couch
- Earth: Rectangular couch

---

4   Tables adapted from course materials, Western School of Feng Shui™.

Complete the table for each element and tally the number for that room. Assess which elements are dominant in the room and which elements may be missing from it. Determine which area of the Bagua the room is in and review the ways the element for that area can be represented. For example, if you are assessing the elements present in your living room, and your living room is in the Wealth and Prosperity area of the Bagua, you want to ensure that the room has a healthy number of representations of Fire and a lesser number of Water, which douses Fire. Include representations of Wood in this area because Wood feeds fire.

The overall goal of the exercise is to achieve a balance of all the Five Feng Shui elements, with a focus on those that enhance each Bagua area.

Water Element   **Room:**

Category	Description	List Items	Total #
Items	Glass, Crystal		
	Mirrors		
	Water features such as fountains		
Art	Depicting waterscapes		
Shapes	Asymmetrical, flowing		
Colors	Black and dark tones		

Total _____

Wood Element   *Room:*

Category	Description	List Items	Total #
Items	Wooden furniture, flooring		
	Anything made of wood		
	Plants (live or artificial)		
	Plant-based cloth (cotton, wool, silk, etc.)		
	Paper, books		
Art	Depicting wooded scenes, flowers		
Shapes	Columnar, stripes		
Colors	Blues and greens		

Total _____

Fire Element　　　　**Room:**

Category	Description	List Items	Total #
Items	All lighting		
	Candles		
	Fireplace		
	Barbecue grill, Fire pit		
	Animal-based items such as fur, feathers		
Art	Depicting people, animals, fire, sun, stars		
Shapes	Triangles, pyramids, cones		
Colors	Red spectrum		

Total _____

Earth Element   ## Room:

Category	Description	List Items	Total #
Items	Tile		
	Adobe and bricks		
	Earthenware		
Art	Depicting landscapes in the earth-tone spectrum		
Shapes	Rectangular, square		
Colors	Yellows and earth tones		

Total   _____

Metal Element　　　*Room:*

Category	Description	List Items	Total #
Items	Made of metal		
	Natural stone		
	Gemstones		
Art	Made of metal, stone, depicting rocky mountains		
Shapes	Circles, arches, ovals		
Colors	White, gray, pastels		

Total _____

As in nature, the Five Elements nurture and control each other. For example, fire melts metal. If you have a room dominated by the Metal element, adding a few enhancements that represent fire, such as a red candle, or art depicting people or animals, can help create balance. Likewise, if you have a room that lacks the Wood element, you could add some flowers (wood) and a fountain, or mirror (water) to further nurture the wood.

Understanding the cycles of the Five Elements will help you bring them into perfect harmony:

To strengthen/nurture elements, follow the nourishing cycle in nature:

- Water helps wood grow.
- Wood is needed to create fire.
- Fire burns to ash and becomes earth.
- Earth over time becomes rocks, which are made into metal.
- Metal can be used to capture and hold water.

To reduce/control elements, follow the controlling cycle in nature:

- Wood creates roots which take over earth.
- Earth stops water from flowing freely.
- Water is used to douse fire.
- Fire turns metal into liquid.
- Metal is used to saw wood.

Recommendations for Creating Balance[5]

- You have too much wood in a room and feel root bound. Add some metal, such as the
- colors white or gray, circular items, and metal items.

---

5   Adapted from course materials, Western School of Feng Shui™.

- You have too little wood in a room and feel you lack creativity. Add some wood and water, such as the colors blue, green, black; plants; and items made of wood.
- You have too much fire in a room and feel stressed, tense, and aggressive. Add some water, such as mirrors, the color black, or items made of glass.
- You have too little fire in a room and feel a lack of positive movement. Add some fire and wood, such as the colors red, blue, and green; items made of wood; or representations of people or animals.
- You have too much earth in a room and feel too conservative and a bit dry. Add some wood, such as a plant, the colors blue or green, or items made of wood.
- You have too little earth in a room and feel spacey. Add some earth and fire, such as the colors yellow and red, rectangular items, and ceramics.
- You have too much metal in a room and feel rigid. Add some fire, such as lighting, something in the color red, pictures of people or animals.
- You have too little metal in a room and feel indecisive. Add some metal and earth, such as the colors white, yellow, gray; circular items; and metal or ceramic items.
- You have too much water in a room and feel a lack of structure. Add some earth, such as yellows and earth tones, rectangles, and ceramics.
- You have too little water in a room and feel a lack of communication. Add some water and metal, such as the colors white, gray, black; circular and metal items; waterscapes, glass, mirrors, and water features.

A Quick Fix: Five-Element Arrangements

Anytime the Five Elements are brought together, they create a positive shift in energy that is both calming and energizing. Creating a small five-element arrangement in a room helps to strengthen the Ch'i and adds power to enhancements and affirmations. It initiates positive change and invites the Ch'i to move. For example, adding a five-element arrangement to the center of your home can help ground you when you are feeling overwhelmed or tired. It is also an excellent strategy to use when you need to boost the energy to new endeavors, such as seeking a job, deciding to start a family, or beginning a large remodeling project. When you feel overwhelmed and don't know where to start with an area, I recommend placing a five-element display in the center of the room to begin moving the Ch'i.

I advised a client whose home was undergoing major reconstruction to place a small table displaying all the Five Elements in her Helpful People and Travel area with an affirmation. She called me to say that after doing this, all stages of the construction went very smoothly. When my husband and I had our deck redone, I took my own advice and created a five-element display by placing a glass vase (water) holding a yellow flower (wood and earth) on top of a metal tray (metal) and adding a red fan (fire).

I placed this Five-Element display in my Helpful People and Travel area for more support. The project went smoothly, our contractors were wonderful, and the deck looks beautiful.

I did the same thing when we were having our kitchen and master bath remodeled, both of which created a great deal of active chaos. To calm the chaos each day after the contractors left, I placed a five-element display on the floor in the center of the room. Immediately the room felt calmer. I removed the display each morning before the contractors arrived. This helped make the remodeling process run smoothly and was much more pleasant for me.

On the kitchen floor I placed a black vase (water) holding two white and red silk orchids (fire, wood, and metal) sitting on a rectangular yellow cloth (earth). Since the kitchen is in the Love, Marriage, and Relationships area, I also placed two lovebirds on the cloth to help enhance love.

Figure 49 Five-Element display in a kitchen remodel

On the bathroom floor I placed a round metal vase (metal) holding two yellow and red silk orchids (wood, earth, and fire) sitting on a yellow rectangular cloth (earth). Next to it I placed two glass candle holders (water and fire). Because the contractors had removed the toilet temporarily and covered the hole with a board, I replaced the board with a rectangular tray to support the arrangement and keep negative energy out.

Figure 50 Five-Element display in a bathroom remodel

When I teach my classes, I assign five-element displays as homework for my students. I love watching their creativity as they bring in floral arrangements, pottery, art, and fabric. Sometimes they even wear the Five Elements. One day a student wore black pants (water) and a green top with red and yellow flowers (wood, fire, earth), accessorized with silver and gold jewelry (metal).

Whatever you add to a room should be purposeful and balanced with the other elements in the room to create harmony. Think of all the different combinations you can, using the things you love.

Balancing the Yin Yang Energy of Your Home or Business

Our universe is made up of opposing forces which the ancient Chinese called Yin and Yang. They can be seen in the examples of night and day, dark and light, large and small, hot and cold. Yin is represented by the earth and the moon and is associated with feminine qualities. Yang is represented by the sky and sun and is associated with masculine qualities. Neither is better nor more important than the other, but a balance of both qualities makes for nurturing environments that help us feel comfortable and thrive.

The following chart of descriptors from The Western School of Feng Shui™6 will help you assess each room in your home for its balance of Yin and Yang. I teach this list of descriptors in my Feng Shui classes and find that it helps students as well as clients recognize the balance or imbalance of these forces in their environments. Use this chart to identify the Yin and Yang qualities in a room and determine whether they need balancing. The key to assessing Yin Yang balance is how comfortable you feel in the room.

Feng Shui Yin Yang Features	Yin Qualities	Yang Qualities
Room size	Small	Large
Location in House	Quiet/Private	Noisy/Busy
Room's View	Intimate/Private	Grand
Room's View	Natural	Houses/Buildings/Street
Ceiling	Low	High
Natural Light	Low	Bright
Electrical Light	Dim	Bright
Open Floor Space	Small Amounts	Large Expanses
Floors	Carpeting/Rugs	Tile/Cement/Stone
Wall Colors	Medium/Dark/Muted	Light/Bright

6   From course materials, Western School of Feng Shui™. All Rights Reserved.

Furniture	Many Pieces	Few Pieces
Furniture Colors	Medium/Dark/Muted	Light/Bright
Furniture and Décor	Small	Large
Furniture and Décor	Low	High
Seating	Soft/Padded	Hard/Unpadded
Furniture Shapes	Curved/Rounded	Straight/Angular
Patterns	Floral	Geometric
Fabrics	Textured	Smooth/Shiny
Design	Elaborate/Ornate	Plain/Uncomplicated
Display Collections	Many	Few/None
Art	Many Pieces	Few
Art	Small	Large
Pillows	Many	Few
Books	Many	Few
Mirrors	Small	Large
Plants	Many	Few
Storage Areas/Closets	Organized	Chaotic/Disorganized

Graphic used by permission from the Western School of Feng Shui™

Yin and Yang qualities are yours to choose based on your preference. Some people like bright, expansive spaces, while others prefer darker, cozy spaces. It is important that you recognize where you are most comfortable. Most people enjoy a balance of Yin and Yang and will instinctively gravitate to environments where things feel good to them. If a very bright Yang room makes you uncomfortable, you can "Yin it up" by adding darker colors, carpets, plants, pillows, pictures, and so on. The same is true if you feel ill at ease in a dark, crowded room. You can "Yang it up" by increasing the lighting and removing some items, as well as substituting lighter colored furniture, walls, and window treatments.

Feng Shui at Work

We had an interior room as a home office. Although it had been elementally balanced to control all the wood, it had no windows, low lighting, and consequently left us feeling tired and stressed by the end of the day. The room was also very small, creating more of a Yin feeling. The solution was painting the walls white and adding a Yang feature in the form of a "light tube" in the ceiling. This is an inexpensive form of skylight that lets in a lot of natural light. The increased light made the room feel bigger, and with the white walls, it felt more Yang. My husband and I have more energy, and love working in our office now.

Usually, different rooms serve different purposes in our lives, and for this reason may inherently be more Yin or Yang, depending on what we intend to draw from them. I have a large great room, which is very Yang, with a lot of natural light and high ceilings. Because of the dark rounded furniture, plants, and numerous personal pictures and items I've displayed around the room, it feels balanced and is a source of renewing energy for me. It is the central hub of my home, and where I do the majority of my entertaining. I love being in this room. My bedroom, however, is more Yin, which feels cozy to me. With its lower ceiling, lower lighting, dark wooden furniture, and burgundy accents, this is the room I spend every evening relaxing, decompressing, and feeling nurtured in. I balanced the Yin by painting the walls a light mushroom color, hanging a large piece of art, and bringing in a tall ficus tree. The armoire is also a very large angular piece of furniture.

There is no right or wrong. Balancing Yin and Yang is not about changing the whole room; sometimes you just need to add or subtract a few items to create the effect you want. As illustrated by the light tube example, small changes can make a big difference. There are those of us who know how to strike a balance naturally, but if you're not sure you do, use the preceding chart as a guide to recognizing the Yin and Yang qualities in your spaces and to determine what adjustments you might make to balance them. If you already have a balanced room, enjoy it! Only make changes if you do not feel comfortable.

Your Turn

Create your own five-element display. What could you use to represent:

Water:

Wood:

Fire:

Earth:

Metal:

Where would you place this display to create an energy shift in your life?

How would you describe your preference in the Yin/Yang spectrum?

Conclusion

Using this workbook format, you have now completed enhancing your first area of need for maximum energy flow, applying all the tools of Feng Shui laid out here:

- Mapping your home using the Bagua
- Identifying the areas of your life that are not working
- Locating those areas on your home's Bagua map and selecting one area to begin working in
- Clearing clutter and revitalizing the space with the placement of meaningful items and personal affirmations
- Balancing the Five Elements and Yin and Yang energy.

You are now ready to return to Chapter 2 to enhance yet another area of need as you continue your journey to empowerment and achieving your goals through Feng Shui, creating a calm, harmonious flow of vital Ch'i energy throughout your home. Continuing to apply Feng Shui principles, you will bring order from chaos, stay grounded, grow in good health and prosperity, and be reminded daily of what you are grateful for.

Feng Shui at Work

A friend had been single for over twenty-five years. She was content with her life, but something was missing. She came to one of my Feng Shui classes and learned that her spacious master bedroom, which she had given over to her three boys, was in the Love, Marriage, and Relationships corner of her home. The boys had since grown, and the room lay empty while she slept in a smaller room at the front of the house. Her life was symbolically empty, waiting for Feng Shui to help her fill it. After learning in class how to enhance her Love, Marriage, and Relationships area, she enthusiastically moved back into the well-lit nurturing space and painted it a warm peach color. She accented with burgundy and added items in pairs and other representations of romance. The view from her bedroom was of a striking burgundy cherry tree which matched the painting of a couple dancing that hung on her wall. The healthy, upward growing tree signified the growth of love. She was living in her own vision board! Soon after wrapping herself in this loving embrace of positive Ch'i, she went on vacation to Costa Rica with a girlfriend, where she met a recently widowed man who quickly became the love of her life. They found each other! After some long-distance dating, they bought a stunning home together and got married. Being Feng Shui converts, they requested a consultation for their new home, where positive Ch'i continues to flow.

This is one of my favorite success stories of people who have used Feng Shui principles to achieve their life goals and realize their dreams. Their stories can be yours, too. Designing your spaces for the vital energy Ch'i to flow purposefully and unimpeded throughout your home or business will bring beauty and harmony into your life and leave you open to new opportunities. Your visualizations will become reality.

Last time our ten-year-old grandson visited, he said to me, "Grandma, I love your home. It's so calm and beautiful." Little did he know he was commenting on Feng Shui at work!

I have always believed in a step-by-step, "salami—slicing off one piece at a time" approach to life, and this book represents my approach to practicing Feng Shui. Take it one step at a time to avoid getting overwhelmed. Begin by prioritizing what's working and not working in your life. Start with one room. Once your applied Feng Shui begins to move the Ch'i, you will see and feel its positive effects. Then turn to another area to begin the process again. Each time it will get easier, until you have achieved the harmony and balance in your environment that will help you achieve your goals. I wish you many Feng Shui blessings as you embark on your journey. Enjoy the unfolding of your harmonious and empowered life!

Appendix 1:
Quick Guide to Bagua Area Enhancements

A client recently told me how helpful the Bagua is. She said it makes shopping and decorating so easy. If she needs to purchase an item, she consults the Bagua, checks colors and shapes, and adds or removes items accordingly. She loves that by using this process, "There are no random acts of decorating." She loves the way her house feels and how it supports her and her life.

What follows is a summation of everything you have learned in Chapter 5 for enhancing the Ch'i in the Bagua areas of your home. Take it with you shopping or use it as a quick reference as you travel on your journey into Feng Shui.

Career (Front Center)

Enhance with:
- Colors: black or very dark colors
- Shapes: asymmetrical
- Items: glass or crystal, mirrors, career images, symbols
- Art: depicting water scenes; flowing water such as rivers, waterfalls, oceans

Knowledge and Self-Cultivation (Front Left Corner)

Enhance with:
- Colors: blues, greens, black
- Shapes: vertical stripes
- Items: wooden; healthy plants with rounded soft leaves; images and symbols of knowledge such as books; representation of deities, inspiring people
- Art: depicting forest scenes, nature scenes, mountains, peaceful places

Health, Family and Friends (Middle Left)

Enhance with:
- Colors: blues, greens
- Shapes: stripes, columns
- Items: healthy floral arrangements; items in wood, photos of family, friends, or representing perfect health
- Art: depicting vibrant flowers

Wealth and Prosperity (Back Left Corner)

Enhance with:
- Colors: purple, blue, red
- Shapes: cones, triangles
- Items: items that "call the Ch'i," such as flags, wind chimes, whirligigs; flowing water features (fountains, waterfalls, aquariums); opulent items in the purple color spectrum; healthy round-leaf plants

- Art: depicting wealth, abundance, such as pictures of lavish houses, boats, cars, family heirlooms or gatherings; art in shades of purple, such as a picture of a lavender field

Fame and Reputation (Back Center)

Enhance with:
- Colors: reds
- Shapes: cones, triangles
- Items: diplomas, awards, and acknowledgments, uplighting, inspirational sayings
- Art: depicting fame, such as famous people, celebrations, toasting, dancers, winners, animals, people, fire, the sun

Love, Marriage, and Relationships (Back Right Corner)

Enhance with:
- Colors: reds, pinks, white
- Shapes: cones, triangles
- Items: candles, lovebirds, hearts, vases in pairs
- Art: objects, paintings, or photos of your significant other, depicting romance or pairs such as flowers, animals, couples

Children and Creativity (Middle Right)

Enhance with:
- Colors: white and pastels
- Shapes: curves and circles
- Items: creative images and symbols, whimsical items, toys, stuffed animals, arts and | crafts supplies, photos of children, metal objects
- Art: whimsical art or art made by children

Helpful People and Travel (Front Right Corner)

Enhance with:

- Colors: white, black, gray
- Shapes: curves, circles
- Items: spiritual images and symbols; metal, natural rocks, stone, and things that remind you of travel
- Art: depicting spiritual guides, mentors, helpful people, or desired travel locations; pictures of mountains

Center and Grounding (Center of Your Home)

Enhance with:

- Colors: yellow, earth tones
- Shapes: squares, rectangles
- Items: ceramics, tiles, bricks
- Art: anything depicted in earth tones such as deserts, wheat fields, yellow trees, sunflowers, or depicting squares or rectangles

Appendix 2:
Special Ch'i Flow Corrections

In Feng Shui there are not many hard and fast rules, but rather recommendations. The most important thing is that you live with what you love. But in areas
that can specifically drain you of vital life energy, there are a few rules that help
to create a more balanced environment and hence a more balanced life. In
an ideal environment, the Ch'i enters through the threshold or your front door
(the "mouth of Ch'i") and continuously flows happily and slowly through the
house, moving in a circular direction, through each of the Bagua areas, back
to the center and around again. It does not get trapped in closets, stumble
over clutter, shoot through windows, get pulled down toilets, or rush down
stairways. But, if due to structural imbalances these things do occur, there are
specific Feng Shui "cures" or corrections that can get the vital energy flowing
freely again. Examples of these cures include the following:

Exposed Ceiling Beams

Although exposed beams are a popular design feature, they are usually
constructed to hold considerable structural weight and can symbolize burdens.
Dark beams can be disconcerting and detract from a peaceful feeling in
the home.

Corrections for Beams. To give beams a lighter visual presence, I recommend
painting the beams and ceiling the same light color. If painting is not an option,
practitioners also recommend hanging soft fabric swags or string lights from
each beam to counterbalance their heaviness.

I slept in the room pictured below at an Airbnb while traveling. The heavy
beams affected my sleep all night. When we returned home, I had a designer
edit the photographs of the room to make them white. You can see in the second
picture the difference it made in softening the feel of the room.

Figure 51 Dark wooden beams

Figure 52 Beams painted the same color as ceiling

Feng Shui at Work

A client had just moved into a new home after a stressful divorce and was concerned about the heavy beams in her master bedroom that were painted a dark shade of brown. They looked oppressive. I recommended she lighten and brighten the room by painting it a soft shade of cream with the beams to match. Since the bedroom was in her Love, Marriage, and Relationships area, I also recommended accent enhancements in shades of reds or pinks, hanging romantic art, and displaying pairs of objects (two candles, a pair of lovebirds, two statues, two hearts, etc.) On my follow-up visit, the room had been transformed into a light, airy boudoir. My client expressed how much she now loves this room and that she has started dating again.

Stairways

Figure 53 Stairs facing the front door

Stairs facing a door are problematic because the Ch'i flows down them too quickly, especially if they point toward the front entrance. Picture Ch'i flowing out of your home and taking all of the positive energy out with it.

Corrections for Stairways. If your staircase points toward the front entrance of your home, all is not lost. There are a number of Feng Shui cures that can help the Ch'i remain happily inside your home. The first is to block the Ch'i with a piece of furniture, a plant, or any other sizeable item you can place between the bottom of the stairs and the door. A second option, and the one I use most frequently with my clients, is to hang a mirror above or next to the door facing the stairs. Finally, if there is room, I recommend hanging a thirty millimeter round faceted crystal somewhere above the bottom of the staircase. I also advise my clients to hang any artwork horizontally along the stairs and not stair-stepped down. You don't want to draw attention downward.

Feng Shui at Work

My daughter had purchased a fourplex in Long Beach. At first, she struggled with keeping the units rented and money from flowing out due to maintenance expenses. While visiting, I did a consultation on her building. The most glaring concern was a tall staircase that led right to the front door. Each of the four units was on either side of this staircase. I immediately recommended that she place a mirror above the door facing the stairs to keep the energy within the structure. Because this was the center of the complex, she grounded it with earth-tone art hung in a horizontal row on either side of the staircase. She also slowed the flow of Ch'i by placing a runner with a gold and green flower pattern on the stairs. Since then, all the units have been successfully rented, and all maintenance completed. She was able to sell the fourplex for a sizeable profit, which allowed her to purchase a condo and a house with an adjacent cottage.

Hallways

Like stairs, halls and long corridors can move the Ch'i through your home too fast.

Corrections for Hallways. Slow the Ch'i flowing down a hallway by hanging art and mirrors along the side walls. This can be a fun location for family pictures. You can break up a long hallway with small pieces of furniture, plants, or rugs. These additions help people walk slower, stop to look at the art or pictures, or check themselves out in a mirror. If possible, place something beautiful (other than a mirror) at the end of the hallway. A mirror would act to send the energy back down the hallway. The idea is to keep the energy flowing in one direction, only slower.

Windows: Pathways for Escaping Ch'i

Figure 54 Large plants placed between sliding glass doors and front entrance

Windows bring in natural light and nourish us with the energy of beautiful views. But as with stairways, when they face the front door and are the first thing you see when you enter the home, the Ch'i is pulled too rapidly across the space and out the window. Remember that ideally, we want the Ch'i to flow happily and slowly through the house.

<u>Corrections for Windows</u>. As with stairs facing a doorway that allows the Ch'i to flow out of your home, a front door facing an expanse of glass allows the Ch'i to flow straight out the back. Figure 54 shows a way to correct this. Placing a few plants between the front entrance and the glass doors at the back helps to slow down the flow of Ch'i. Small pieces of furniture can also be placed between the front door and glass opening. If neither of these corrections is an option, a thirty millimeter round faceted crystal can be hung between the door and the glass opening to achieve the same result.

Many houses near where we live have commanding water views. Unfortunately, many are designed so that when you open the front door you are swept away by the breathtaking view that is visible immediately. But so is the Ch'i, right through the house and out the door. Clients with houses like these have experienced financial losses and suffered health issues. Without compromising the view, some have blocked the river of Ch'i from escaping by placing a piece of furniture or a beautiful plant between the front door and the windows. Others have hung a thirty millimeter round faceted crystal somewhere in the room between the door and the window. It is important to find the enhancement that best suits your taste and lifestyle yet keeps the vital energy circulating freely within your home.

As always with Feng Shui, a few common cures will improve the Ch'i flow in your home and have a very direct and empowering effect on your life.

Your Turn

Do you have dark beams in your home? If so, what can you do to soften the look and help the Ch'i flow peacefully?

Do you have a stairway leading to your front door? If so, what can you do to block the Ch'i from flowing out?

Describe your hallways. If they are long, what can you do to slow down the energy flow?

Stand with your back to the inside of your front door. Can you see straight through a picture window or glass door? If so, what can you place between the front door and the glass opening to keep the Ch'i from flowing out?

Acknowledgments

It is said that people come into your life for a reason, a season, or a lifetime. There are those people who touch your life and change it forever. Four incredibly special women entered my life at different times, during transitions, placing me on a course that would lead me to my journey into Feng Shui.

Judy Fruhbauer, one of my gifted teachers while I was principal at Ulatis Elementary School, introduced me to Feng Shui. It was exactly what I needed during the transitional period I was in.

Michelle Cox, the Feng Shui practitioner Judy introduced me to, blessed my home and gave me countless hours of advice, leading me to a loving marriage and career advancement.

Terah Kathryn Collins and Karen Abler-Carrasco, my master teachers and Feng Shui guides through the Western School of Feng Shui™. These wise teachers, whom I had the blessing of meeting more ten years ago at their certification institute, continue to be mentors, spiritual guides, and friends during all of life's transitions.

I am also blessed to have in my life the numerous people who have taken the time to read, review, and edit these pages in their roughest form, offering their sage advice, wisdom, and grammatical knowledge. Thank you to Evie Groch, Terah Kathryn Collins, Katy Colbath, Katrina McCullough, John Furtado and Karen Abler-Carrasco. Thank you also to my fabulous copy editor, Nancy Silk, who helped me condense, clarify, and organize my numerous ideas into a publishable form, and to Kymberli Weed Brady for the cover design and updated headshot. The support and friendship I've received from all of you through this journey has been invaluable.

Blessings.

Bibliography/Recommended Reading

Figure 55 Sculpture of a scribe – gift from Terah Kathryn Collins

Anthony, Carol K. and Hanna Moog. *I Ching: The Oracle of the Cosmic Way*. Stow, Massachusetts: Anthony Publishing, 2002.

Bodin, Luc, M.D., Nathalie Bodin Lamboy, and Jean Graciet. *The Book of Ho'oponopono: The Hawaiian Practice of Forgiveness and Healing*. Rochester, Vermont: Destiny Books, 2016.

Carter, Karen Rauch. *Move Your Stuff, Change Your Life*. New York, New York: Simon and Schuster, 2002.

Collins, Terah Kathryn. *The Western Guide to Feng Shui*. Carlsbad, California: Hay House, 1996.

Collins, Terah Kathryn. *The Western Guide to Feng Shui Room by Room.* Carlsbad, California: Hay House, 1999.

Collins, Terah Kathryn. *Home Design With Feng Shui A–Z.* Carlsbad, California: Hay House, 2001.

Collins, Terah Kathryn. *The Western Guide to Feng Shui for Prosperity.* Carlsbad, California: Hay House, 2002.

Collins, Terah Kathryn. *The Western Guide to Feng Shui for Romance.* Carlsbad, California: Hay House, 2004.

Collins, Terah Kathryn. *The Three Sisters of the Tao.* Carlsbad, California: Hay House, 2010.

Grillo, Lorrie Webb. *Yin Yang and Prosper.* Denver, Colorado: Thriving Spaces, 2020.

Rossbach, Sarah. *Interior Design with Feng Shui.* New York, New York: Arkana Books, 1987.

Rubin, Gretchen. *The Happiness Project.* New York, New York: Harper Collins, 2009.

Silver, Tosha. *Outrageous Openness.* New York, New York: Atria Paperback, Simon & Schuster, 2014.

"Earl Nightingale Quotes." *BrainyQuote,* 1921–1989. https://www.brainyquote.com/authors/earl-nightingale-quotes

About the Author

Maria McCullough

Maria McCullough is the owner/founder of **Feng Shui by Maria** (www.fengshuibymaria.com). She is a graduate of the Western School of Feng Shui™, which teaches the art of Essential Feng Shui®—the practical study of how to arrange your environment to enhance your life. Maria is trained in residential, business, and landscape consultations. She offers virtual consultations nationally and internationally, as well as in person locally.

She has always had a passion for interior design. Born in Milan, Italy, Maria was influenced by her multilingual, artistic parents who immigrated to this country from Europe. Although she majored in interior design at Cal Poly State University at San Luis Obispo, Maria chose a rewarding career in education, finishing her graduate work at Cal State Hayward. For more thirty-five years she worked with children and adults as a teacher, and later as an educational administrator, with a focus on instructional excellence.

As a lifelong learner, Maria has been fascinated with the study of Feng Shui for more than twenty years, being introduced to it by one of her teachers when she was an elementary school principal. She has held numerous consultations in her home and office, read a variety of books about Feng Shui, and studied with Feng Shui practitioners Michelle Cox, Terah Kathryn Collins, and Karen Abler-Carrasco. She teaches classes locally and is a Feng Shui columnist for the *Benicia Herald*. She is a former columnist for the *Martinez News Gazette* and *Contra Costa County Community Focus* newspapers.

Experiencing firsthand the positive difference Feng Shui made in her own life, Maria developed a true passion for sharing her knowledge with those closest to her. Combining her love of teaching with her passion for Feng Shui, she now brings those experiences to others and delights in their successful life improvements!

Testimonial:

"As soon as I started making the enhancements that Maria recommended for my home, I felt the energy shift both inside my home and inside me. Maria took the time to get to know me and my vision for my life so that she could personalize her recommendations and align them with my dreams and goals. She prepared a detailed list of enhancements that is easy to follow and easy to complete one item at a time, so you don't get overwhelmed. One of my dreams is to marry my soul mate, and within months of beginning to make Maria's enhancements, I was engaged! I believe that the new energy in my home helps to make him feel welcome and loved and "at home" and helped magnetize him to me. I highly recommend Maria's services to help all of your dreams come true!"